Praise for
"If You Do Nothing, You'll Die"

"Posey had me at her description of being in the grocery store and wondering how everyone else could be simply going about their day while her world was crashing in. Her story is described in vivid detail with honesty and humor. For anyone who has made this journey, or has had life change in an instant, this is an important read."

Lee Woodruff – Author of *In An Instant*

"It is hard to imagine anything worse than severe cognitive impairment, but the one who suffers the most is the caregiver. The loved one is alive, but a markedly different person. In her story of unimaginable loss, Posey demonstrates the courage and humor that helped her survive and grow. It is a testament to the strength of the human spirit and an inspiration and comfort to all who share her journey of pain and dedication to a loved one who can no longer care for himself.
She is open about her failing days and she can eek humor out of just about any situation. The book leaves us with hope, a smile and renewed dedication to solve the big or decidedly smaller challenges that we all face."

Marelene Brusko, Psy.D., Clinical Psychologist

"This book provides profound insight into the day-to-day reality that is brought about by grave changes in thinking and personality and its rippling effects on family and friends."

Christina Blodgett Dycus, PH.D.,
Clinical Neuropsychologist

"We in the medical field, often forget that we treat not just patients with diseases, but the hearts, minds and souls of the families and friends of those who are ill. Eric's story of his brain tumor, so lovingly and beautifully described in these pages by his devoted wife Wendy, serves as a reminder to us of this fact. In the end, this book is a story of hope, faith, and the life-giving power of love. Prepare to be inspired."

George K. Bovis, MD, Neurosurgeon

I will never forget the day I was born and I made a cooing sound on my dad's shoulder and my dad said "I'll sign any thing my mom would put in front of him for me.

Rosie Posey
Daddy
Alex
Daddy
Tommy

Dear Lord please watch over my dad, please make him happy and keep him safe

WE MISS YOU DADDY

I really loved throwing the football with Daddy.

Daddy

Tommy

March 15, 2008

As part of the preparation for Eric's funeral, Alex and Tommy were asked to draw a picture about their Dad and the drawings were included in the funeral mass program.

"IF YOU DO NOTHING, YOU'LL DIE"

"IF YOU DO NOTHING, YOU'LL DIE"

One Wife's Story of Love, Brain Surgery
and The Heartbreaking Aftermath

WENDY L. POSEY

TŌMEX
PUBLISHING

"If You Do Nothing, You'll Die"
One Wife's Story of Love, Brain Surgery
and The Heartbreaking Aftermath
by Wendy L. Posey

Published by Tomex Publishing
P.O. Box 1116
Palatine, IL 60078 USA
www.tomexpublishing.com

Cover design by Dave Krzeminski
Interior design by Sue Balcer of JustYourType.biz

Published in the United States of America

Publisher's Cataloging-in-Publication
(Provided by Quality Books, Inc.)

    Posey, Wendy L.
       "If you do nothing, you'll die": one wife's story of love, brain surgery and the heartbreaking aftermath / by Wendy L. Posey.
       p. cm.
       LCCN 2009938514
       ISBN-13: 978-0-9825681-6-3
       ISBN-10: 0-9825681-6-9

       1. Posey, Eric W., d.2008. 2. Posey, Wendy L.
    3. Brain--Tumors--Patients--United States--Biography.
    4. Caregivers--United States--Biography. 5. Caregivers'
    writings, American. I. Title.

    RD663.P67 2010   616.99'4'0922
                         QBI09-600214

This book is for…

Eric, my soul mate,

My mom, whose strength, humor and love for her family
was and continues to be an inspiration

and Alex and Tommy, the two greatest blessings of my life.

Table of Contents

Acknowledgements

To my editor, Faye Levow, with whom I felt an instant connection. Thank you for all your hard work. To Shelly Rosenberg, thanks for your attention to detail and your warm compassion. Thank you Sue Balcer for sharing your talent and expertise and providing exceptional interior book design services. Thank you Dave Krzeminski for your wonderful designs and Dana Krzeminski for your help in the early stages of this book.

I dealt with a lot of medical personnel over the course of Eric's illness. He had so many great doctors and therapists. I watched how hard they worked with him and was truly moved by their kindness and dedication.

To my family for all of their support, especially my mom for her endless help and for teaching me to find the humor in things. I miss you everyday.

To Eric's entire family, I am so grateful for all of their support, especially Maggie, who was there with me and my mom in the trenches, through all the craziness and mayhem. Thank you. I love you very much.

To Steve Johnson, thanks for a perfectly timed, unforgettable trip of a lifetime and all the laughs.

Thanks to Regina and Ann for being there during the eye of the storm.

To Sarah Nicolson, Lisa Goldman and everyone at Anixter's New Focus program, I am so appreciative for everything you did to help Eric.

To Sue McTague, for helping Eric tremendously and preserving my sanity. Thank you for thinking of us and for your friendship.

To Jen Gatti and the facilities group at Willow Creek Community Church, and to Norm Canfield and the folks in accounting at the Hyatt Regency Woodfield, thanks for taking a chance on Eric and giving him a purpose. You were all so compassionate and I thank you from the bottom of my heart.

Thank you to Luis and Arturo Diaz for your caring and loving hearts.

To the man we lovingly called "Bill the Blindman," thank you, thank you, thank you!

To my friends at Holy Family Parish, the CFM and choir groups, whose support and acceptance meant so much to me, especially Colin Collette, whose spirit and enthusiasm helped me through many difficult years, thank you. Colin, you are an inspiration to many.

To the phenomenal women I had the honor of spending time with at Miraval. You are all an inspiration.

Don Guinter, D.R. Papalia, Rick Castle and Rob Reichley, thank you for being such incredible friends to Eric.

Eric Schmude, there are no words to describe the gratitude I feel toward you. You were the best friend Eric ever had and your loyalty did not, and does not, go unnoticed.

As I wrote in the book, I am lucky to have such amazing friends. Robin, Wendy H., and Katina, I am thankful everyday for your support and your friendship. You are all so much fun and I am lucky to share my life and so many laughs with each of you.

Julie and Maureen, how did I get so lucky? You are caring, genuine, down to earth, funny, giving, quality women who I am proud to call my friends. I am truly blessed.

To Dan Poynter, for making me believe I could write this book, I am so thankful.

Alex and Tommy, know that Daddy is always looking down on you, smiling and is so very proud of you both.

And last, but certainly not least, to Eric, you are loved and missed.

Foreword

In the five years that our 43 year old son Eric suffered his "benign" brain tumor, life as his mother changed for me. This child, who grew to be bright, successful, loving and happy, became passive and remote, a vacant physical echo of himself, a child once again. When he was two, I could help him through the measles; at 12 I could comfort him through the flu and at 17 I could soothe the football bruises. At 43 he had a headache; what does a mother do with a brain tumor? The shock was strange, unthinkable.

Life for him and for us changed.

His dad, Wendy and I sat in the surgical waiting room as families came and went. We sat. Hours. Then days. Then months. And years; it all runs together. All those things you hear: disbelief, anger, fear and tears. Where does my strength come from? Wendy, the girl Eric first told me had "curly hair. No, Mom. I mean really curly hair" was my gift. She and I have formed a bond beyond mother and daughter-in-law. In stunned grief we cried, laughed, nurtured two beautiful children and to this day have a tie that is secure. Her book tells the story that she and so many brothers, cousins, and friends have shared. Looking back at all that has happened I do believe that each mother has the instinct to endure the pain of losing a child. She will find her way.

– Marjorie E. Posey

Preface

"If you do nothing, you'll die." That was quite an opening line, considering it was the first time we ever met Dr. T. These were his first words after he looked at Eric's x-rays on the light-up board in the conference room. Eric and I sat in stunned silence.

What a journey we were on - from the uncertainty of the exhausting hospital months to the hilarity and gut-wrenching sadness of some of the rehab sessions. It feels strange putting in writing that Eric is gone. To say that we miss him is the biggest understatement in the world. In my head, I am grateful that he is finally out of his misery and no longer suffering, but in my heart, I ache endlessly, wishing he were still here - the healthy Eric, that is.

I met my soul mate when I met Eric, all those years ago. I treasure every step of the journey we had together. When I am very sad, I try to remind myself how lucky I was to share my life with such an amazing man.

I'm a believer that everything happens for a reason. You may not find out the reason for a long time or maybe ever, but I think there's always a reason. As for me, maybe I needed to learn patience or maybe I needed some perspective. Maybe this happened to us so we could, in turn, help others. Who knows?

My wish is that if life has thrown you some curveballs, you find hope and strength in our story, and learn that it is possible to make it through. Take comfort that you are not alone in your feelings and thoughts as you deal with the enormous challenges life has given you.

–Wendy L. Posey

PART ONE

In The Beginning, There Were Headaches...

Looking for the Cause

IT ALL STARTED WITH HEADACHES. I wasn't surprised Eric was having headaches; he was under a lot of stress. He had just started a new job two months prior, after being let go from his previous job of 18 years. He found his new position after 10 months of searching and was working hard, setting up his new office, and establishing himself.

At first, the headaches were minor. Eric never even mentioned them. I would notice him rubbing his forehead or I'd hear the cabinet open and the aspirin bottle shake. Only if asked, would Eric confirm that he had a headache. One day, I picked up the giant Costco-sized bottle of aspirin and was surprised how light it was, knowing it hadn't been very long since I'd bought it. Eventually, when we were sleeping, Eric would groan in pain from headaches. Aspirin would always help.

Eric also was having trouble with his right field of vision. When he read the newspaper he would get to the middle of a sentence and the rest of the sentence would disappear. He had to move his whole head to the right in order to see the rest of the sentence. I thought he needed to go to the eye doctor because he wore glasses and maybe needed a new prescription. Eventually, the pain got so bad that Eric's groaning was accompanied by rolling around in bed, trying to withstand the pain.

He went to the eye doctor on a Tuesday evening and Wednesday morning we got a call from our regular doctor. Dr. P told us that the eye doctor recommended an MRI and a CT scan to help find the cause for the headaches. He also requested that I make a follow-up appointment with him three days later, so he could review the resulting films and reports with us.

Eric had the tests the following Tuesday evening and I was happy that we would have our follow-up appointment in three days to find out what this was all about.

Just a Normal Family Life

THE DAY AFTER ERIC HAD THE MRI and CT scan was a hectic, typical Wednesday morning in our house. Alex, our 3-year-old daughter, and Tommy, our 10-month-old son, were upstairs in our bedroom with me, screaming and wrestling with each other as I made our bed and prepared to take a shower.

Eric had already had breakfast and had left for the office. The day's schedule began with "Terrific 3's," a one-hour park district class that Alex really enjoyed, while I walked the jogging track in the gym with Tommy in the stroller.

The morning routine always felt like military maneuvers, getting both kids and myself, fed, dressed and out the door. It was 8:00 a.m. and class didn't start for two hours. Dare I say we would be on time that day?

The TV seemed to be getting louder as I picked up the toys, stuffed animals and books that always made their way into our room. Over the blare of "Blue's Clues," I heard the phone ring.

"Hello?"

"Is this Mrs. Posey?"

"Yes it is."

"This is Dr. P. Is Eric home?"

"No, Eric is at the office. We just had the tests you ordered done last night at 8:30 p.m. and we have an appointment to see you Friday morning."

The doctor's voice was faint, although it just could have been "Blue's Clues" getting louder. "Yes," he said, "I know you had the tests last night. That's why I'm calling. I have the results and it's not good news." He asked if he should tell me and then call Eric at the office.

Maybe I wasn't fully awake yet, but I wasn't grasping the gravity of the phone call. I said, "Yes, tell me."

The doctor said, "Eric has a mass in his brain."

This is the night of Cinderella's Ball, a daddy/daughter dance, eleven days before surgery.

I am a long time loyal fan of the soap opera "All My Children." There goes any credibility I may have had. What can I say? Some people drink, some use drugs, I watch All My Children.

A lot has happened to the folks in Pine Valley, Pennsylvania, the fictional town that is the setting for "All My Children," home of cosmetics diva and many times married, Erica Kane. If I were a resident of Pine Valley, upon hearing Dr. P's words, "Eric has a mass in his brain," there would have been a musical organ tone, low and deep... "dum dum dum dum..." as I stared off with my mouth agape. There was no background music, but I probably had the stare.

I remember leaning back on the bedroom wall, hearing the doctor's words and slowly sliding to the ground, ending in a crouched position, still clutching the phone. Eric has a mass in his brain. *A mass in his brain.* That sounded big, so I asked.

"How big is it?"

"Big," replied Dr. P.

"How big?" I repeated.

I could tell he didn't want to tell me, but after some pressing, he said, "Six centimeters."

Now my mind was scrambling. Heck if I could picture what six centimeters looked like. For the love of God, couldn't he have just said it in inches? So I asked, "How big is it in inches?"

He said, "Approximately 2 ½ inches."

I estimated 2 ½ inches with my thumb and forefinger, and then held it up to my forehead. Shock and disbelief washed over me. *Cue the organ music.* That's a big mass to be in someone's brain, let alone my husband's brain.

I asked the doctor, "Is this a brain tumor?"

He said, "Yes."

I asked him what we should do.

He calmly gave me the phone number to a neurosurgeon and told me to call when we hung up. "Tell them you have to get in today for a consultation. Pick up the films from the MRI and CT scan done last night and bring them to the appointment."

That was the mind-blowing part of all this. Eleven hours ago, Eric and I were sitting at the local hospital at 9:00 p.m. for tests and now it was 8:00 a.m. and our doctor was calling us with the results. Usually you have to hunt down doctors, re-explain who you are and promise to give up your first-born to get any action. The fact that our first call that morning was the doctor, drove home the fact that this was serious…no organ music needed.

I am a very strong person, not so much physically, although I can hold my own, but emotionally. I always have been. I attribute it to "strong genes." My mom was the strongest person I ever knew. She suffered more heartache and loss than anyone should ever have to endure in one lifetime and she faced it all with unwavering strength and class.

When I found out my husband, Eric, had a brain tumor, I needed every ounce of strength I could muster and then some. Not only did I need to be strong, but as I wrote this book, I was amazed at the amount of patience I had… well, most of the time.

The news was shocking. No doubt about it. But I figured we'd do what we had to do to take care of it and move on. I mean, how bad could it be? *A piece of advice from me to you: Don't ever ask yourself, "How bad could it be?" unless you're prepared for the answer.*

I quickly switched to "fix-it" mode. I used to work at a company where the Chief Financial Officer used to say, "Bad news does not improve with age." *Very true.*

After I slid down the bedroom wall, I started making the appointments and phone calls to inform our families. From that moment, it felt like I didn't stop moving for many years.

It's a fascinating story. *Even more so if it weren't my husband we were talking about.* The things my family has endured along the way have been terrifying, joyous, maddening, sad, hysterically funny, depressing and very surreal. The journey was exhausting, draining and one I wouldn't wish on anyone.

My hope is that this book will help someone who may be experiencing or has experienced the "loss" of a loved one who is not deceased, but altered.

I hope to connect with caregivers caring for loved ones who are no longer the people they once were. I hope readers gain strength from my story and know they are not alone in their thoughts and feelings. I hope too that doctors gain some insight into what happens in their patients' lives once their 15-minute appointment is over.

Alex and Tommy, a little over a month before Eric's tumor was diagnosed. I forgot how little they were.

The Last Supper

I FOLLOWED DR. P'S DIRECTIONS. He called Eric at the office and I called the neurosurgeon and set up an appointment for 4:00 that same day.

The next incoming call was from Eric. He said, "What do you think?"

I told him that I thought it was scary, but I had already made the appointment with the neurosurgeon and we'd get it taken care of.

I asked Eric what he was thinking and he said he didn't know what to think. He said, "We'll just have to wait and see what the surgeon has to say."

What he had to say was scary. But first I had to throw a tantrum at the window of the records department because they weren't going to give us the test films to take to the appointment. Since the tests were just run the night before, they hadn't made copies of the films yet. I threatened some lives, signed a release and off we went to our appointment.

After reviewing the films very briefly, the doctor told us that they didn't handle surgeries like ours in a community hospital. He said we would have to go to a university hospital, where they had a team of surgeons to handle this type of surgery. *Oh my God. A team of surgeons? What is happening here?*

Then he picked up the phone and called a doctor at the local University Medical Center. After waiting a while for the doctor to come to the phone, we heard our doctor say that he had a couple in his office, Mr. and Mrs. Posey. "Mr. Posey presented with headaches and his MRI is showing a mass in his brain of blah blah blah size, consistent with blah blah blah." *Seriously...that is what it sounded like to me.*

When he hung up, we had an appointment with that doctor the following day at 4:00 p.m. He told us this doctor was a well-respected neurosurgeon, who would review Eric's films and advise as to the best plan of action.

This whole thing was really scaring us. We knew that Eric was having terrible headaches and we knew he had a brain tumor, but beyond that, we'd just have to wait to meet with the Dr. from the university hospital.

Our friends, Robin and Mike, watched Alex and Tommy for us while we went to the appointment. The drive to the university hospital was long. We followed the directions and traffic was heavy. *Little did I know then that I would soon be able to make the drive practically blindfolded.*

We met in the building next to the hospital, where the doctor had his office. We were shown into the conference room to wait for the doctor. There was a long wood conference table with a box of Kleenex on it. It was eerily quiet and we waited in silence for what seemed like forever.

Dr. T walked in and introduced himself and his assistant. The doctor was tall and had a commanding, confident presence. His assistant took a seat across from us, while the doctor put Eric's x-rays on a light-up board on the wall for all of us to see. Standing next to the x-rays, he delivered his attention-getting opening line, "If you do nothing, you'll die."

The doctor pointed to various parts of the x-ray and explained that the location of the tumor was in the frontal lobe of the brain, sitting on the optic nerves. *That explains why Eric was losing his right field of vision.*

The doctor said that the tumor was very large and in an area of the brain that houses <u>memory</u> and <u>personality</u>. He said surgery was needed to remove the tumor and it should be done sooner than later. *Oh my God...oh my God.*

The whole time Dr. T was talking, he was staring just at me—talking directly to me. I was pre-occupied because I thought to myself, *Oh my gosh, he thinks I'm the one with the tumor. Maybe I should interrupt and tell him that it's not me, it's Eric.* Later, my mom told me that he was staring at me because he knew I was the one who would be dealing with the aftermath of the surgery.

The doctor said there was a series of tests that needed to be done before surgery. He spoke to his assistant about various surgeries, appointments, and clinics that he could re-schedule to accommodate Eric's surgery.

The doctor spoke slowly and deliberately and explained that because of the location of the tumor, there could be a change in personality. I made a joke and said, "Hey, while you're in there can you tweak a few things?"

The doctor didn't crack a smile; he just stared right at me. *He probably knew I wouldn't be making jokes later.* He also said we should be prepared for Eric to be out of work for as long as one year. *If only the doctor's prediction was right.*

Dr. T told us that his nurse would write up the orders for the pre-surgery tests, which could be done on an outpatient basis. Also, they would let us know when surgery would be scheduled.

He stressed, before he left the room, that this was a big surgery and that we should take the time to think of any necessary arrangements we might need to make. *Arrangements? I'm too young to have to make any kind of arrangements. On the way out I took a Kleenex for the road. Gulp.*

We picked up some sandwiches on the way home and ate with Mike and Robin. We told them about the appointment. To this day, Mike and Robin refer to that casual dinner as "the last supper." The last time they saw Eric as they knew him—before surgery.

One Week Before Surgery

THE WEEK BEFORE ERIC'S SURGERY, we completed all the necessary paperwork, "our arrangements," as Dr. T said. My friend, Julie, referred us to one of her colleagues to draw up a will, a property power of attorney, and health care power of attorney for each of us. What a surreal experience.

Normally when you make these kinds of arrangements, the scenario is always "just to be covered" in case an unlikely event might occur many years down the road. For us, Eric was one week away from brain surgery and the doctor told us to make our arrangements. Ahhhhh!

Since it was February, we made an appointment and got our taxes done; he was the same guy Eric had used for many years even before we met. His office was not conveniently located in relation to where we lived, but we figured we only went once a year, so we could make the drive.

Eric usually did all the driving when we were together. My problem was that if I wasn't driving, I'd never pay attention to how we got to our destination, even if we went many times. This drove Eric crazy. He'd say, "What do you mean you don't know how to get there, we've been going there for ten years?"

On this day, when we went to get our taxes done the week before Eric's brain surgery, I wrote the directions down on the inside cover of our tax file, so I would know how to get there in the future, if I needed to. It was a good thing I did.

Eric's biggest concern was that he didn't want to be a third "kid" whom I had to care for. That was his only concern. He had no real fear. When I asked him if he was scared, he told me that he didn't know what to expect or what to be afraid of. Everyone else was acting how I thought Eric should have been acting. Eric was demonstrating almost an eerie calm.

His parents came to stay with us the week before surgery, while we completed all the "pre-surgery" tests. Eric's father was very worried and upset. Eric told me he had only seen his dad cry twice in his life, when each of his parents died. Now his dad seemed to be welling up every time I looked at him.

Eric said the same thing to his dad that he said to everyone else: There was no choice in the matter. He had to have the surgery or he'd die, so that was what he was going to do.

His dad kept marveling at how bravely Eric was facing the surgery and cried when he talked to Eric about it. I watched Eric console his father and tell him not to worry. *Pretty ironic, the patient consoling the family.*

One of the pre-surgical tests was a brain angiogram. As explained to me, it served as a roadmap for the neurosurgeon when he was doing the surgery. The kid who conducted the angiogram, (*I say "kid" because suddenly, all the doctors on "the team" looked too young to be admitted into an "R" rated movie, let alone be conducting tests on my husband's brain*) made a remark that he was surprised Eric wasn't blind or unconscious due to the size and location of the tumor. *Great.*

The night before surgery, when we went to bed, Eric told me he was scared of all the unknown things. Would he live to see our two beautiful kids grow up? And if he did live, would he end up being a burden on me? Again, a third kid to be taken care of.

I told him I was scared, too, but we would get through this together. I told him he couldn't die because I would kill him!

Eric always told me he loved me, every night before we went to bed, and he'd say it the same way every time. "I love you Wendy, more than you'll ever know," and this is what he said to me this night, the night before his brain surgery.

Day of Surgery – 2/25/03
And The End of Life as I Had Known It

WE HAD TO BE AT THE HOSPITAL at 5:30 a.m. the day of surgery. We were put in our own curtained-off cubbyhole; the other cubbies were occupied by all the other people having morning surgery. The typical things you'd expect took place. They took Eric's blood pressure, listened to his heart, and started a port so they could hook up the IV during surgery.

I helped Eric change into his gown and they gave me a clear plastic bag with the hospital's name in blue letters to keep the patient's clothes and personal belongings.

Sitting in the pre-surgery holding area, Eric and I had already said everything important that needed to be said. Eric was lying on a bed and I was sitting on the edge, holding his hand. We were nervous. We made small talk about the operating room and anesthesia and the kids and home and what time family members were going to be coming to the hospital during the course of the day.

A girl in scrubs approached us and said they were going to move Eric to the pre-surgery area. When we were finally rolling down the hall and I was walking alongside Eric in the bed, the girl steering informed me that this was where I had to say goodbye and go wait in the family waiting room for the doctor to talk to us before surgery.

I thought Eric and I would have more time together before surgery. There we stood saying our goodbyes in the middle of the hall, while Eric lay on the bed. The girl just stood there while I kissed Eric goodbye and told him I loved him and to be strong. I could feel my voice getting quivery and my eyes starting to fill up and didn't want Eric to see me crying just before he went into brain surgery. *There's a real pick-me-up. Eric would think, great, my wife is crying… she probably thinks I'm a goner!* I kept my emotions together, but felt like our "goodbye" was so abrupt.

The girl who was pushing Eric's bed seemed impatient, practically tapping her foot, while I said goodbye to my husband who was going to have his head opened and his brain sliced up. I waved to him until the bed turned the corner and was out of sight. That was the last time I spoke to the Eric I knew—the man I fell in love with and married.

The family waiting room was dark and empty. It was only 6:30 a.m. The room contained loveseats, couches, chairs, and coffee tables forming many small conversation pits. There was a TV mounted in the air in the corner of the room, a desk, and a credenza that had a coffee maker on it, but no pot or coffee was to be seen.

I sat down on one of the chairs, holding my brand spanking new address book and waited. We had a typical overused address book; pages falling out, slips of paper thrown in with the good intention of transferring the information into the book, but it never happened. Now that I had seven hours on my hands with nothing to do but wait, it was the perfect activity to pass the time.

I was the first one in the family waiting room, but as time passed, people began arriving, one-by-one, holding clear plastic bags containing their loved one's personal effects.

At 8:00 a.m. a perky, little, old, white-haired lady, who was all smiles, walked into the waiting room wearing a pink smock with a pin that read "volunteer." She proceeded to unlock the credenza and unload all the makings for coffee, as well as a telephone that she plugged into a phone jack near the desk. She placed a candy jar on the desk and made a pot of coffee.

Picking up her clipboard, she asked for everyone's attention, and announced that we all needed to check in with her so she knew what patient's families were here. She explained that as the surgeries were underway, a nurse from the operating room would call the waiting room to update the families on the progress of their loved ones' surgeries. If any of us left the room for any reason, we needed to let her know.

I was amazed at the number of people filling this waiting room. This was one day of one year in one hospital. Who knew how many surgeries were performed in this country on a given day? It seemed that there was no excuse for anyone to have an untidy address book!

Dr. T found me, along with Eric's parents, in the waiting room around 7:30 a.m. He said, "It's going to be a long day." *He has a knack for opening lines.*

He explained that it would take approximately 45 minutes to set up in the operating room and we would get updates about every hour and a half. He estimated it would be a six- to eight-hour surgery and told us he was thinking of keeping Eric in the hospital and doing a second surgery within a week, depending on how much of the tumor was accessible during the first surgery. This was a change. The original plan was to have the first surgery and allow several months for healing before doing surgery again.

We finished our talk with Dr. T and he left, headed for the operating room. *It was strange to think he was going to open up my husband's head and mess with his brain.*

At 8:45 a.m., the phone rang in the waiting room. The little, white-haired lady answered and called out, "Posey family." The nurse from the operating room was on the phone and told me they were getting started.

We got three more updates during the day:

9:50 a.m. – They were working on the tumor and everything was going well.

11:00 a.m. – Still working. Everything going well.

11:50 a.m. – The section of the tumor they were working on was out and they were starting to close.

I wondered if anyone else thought it was bizarre that they called from the operating room with updates. Don't get me wrong, that really helped reduce the stress of waiting, but I just pictured the surgical team hovering over Eric working and one of them leaving to call me in the waiting room.

I spent the day people-watching, one of my favorite past times. I figured out who was with whom and wondered what kind of surgery everyone else's loved one was having. I saw a lot of families come and go while I waited.

2:30 p.m. – Dr. T entered the waiting room and spoke with me and Eric's parents, in a little conference room off to the side. He told us he got 90% of the tumor out and to expect erratic behavior from Eric during the next several weeks. Knowing what I know now, I WISH it just lasted only several weeks.

The doctor explained that emotionally, Eric would be all mixed up and jumbled. He said when Eric wanted to laugh, he may cry and vise versa. Dr. T said that verbally, Eric would be "goofy as a loon." He'd use crazy words and wouldn't make any sense. He told us they'd do an MRI in a few days to see what was left of the tumor and what the next step would be.

4:30 p.m. – We were finally able to see Eric. The sight of him hooked up to all the beeping machines and wires with his head wrapped in gauze, turned my stomach at first glance. There were several nurses hovering over him, busily tending to the machines and tubes. The nurse tested Eric's ability to put pressure on his arms and legs and count the number of fingers the nurse was holding up. He did fine with all three tasks. Eric was trying to pull on his wires so the nurse put loose arm restraints on his arms.

At about 5:30 p.m., approximately one hour after we first walked in to see Eric, he had a grand mal seizure. When the seizure started, Eric's dad and I were at his bedside and his mom happened to be on the other side of the curtain. I have always been grateful she didn't have to witness the seizure. Eric's face was scrunched and twisted and his tongue was slightly out of his mouth, off to the side. His head kept jerking fast, looking straight on and then to the severe right, then back again, over and over. Eric's legs seemed to be moving and his torso was rising up and down off the hospital bed—*a mild Linda Blaire impression.*

I don't remember if I yelled or not, but within seconds there were a bunch of doctors and nurses surrounding Eric. His parents and I were on the other side of the drawn curtain waiting for what seemed like an eternity, but I'm sure it was only a few minutes.

One of the team doctors told us that Eric had a grand mal seizure that lasted 45 seconds. He said Eric's oxygen level never dropped during the seizure, so there was no need to worry about brain damage.

Although anti-seizure medication had already been given to Eric, obviously it wasn't enough, so they loaded him up with it and said he'd sleep through the night.

I went back home with Eric's parents and called the ICU for an update around 9:30 that night. Again, they told me that Eric was very exhausted and would sleep through the night. This seemed like the longest day of my life. Little did I know then, that it was the first day of a three and a half-month-long hospital stay and the beginning of the end of life as we knew it.

It was strange going to bed that night in our king-sized bed by myself. You get used to the other person always being there. My mind raced with all that happened that day. I kept wondering what the outcome would be. My last thought before I went to sleep was that I had never opened my brand-spanking-new address book. So much for being organized.

In the Hospital—Secret Stairways & Doctor Sightings

THE HOSPITAL PHASE OF ERIC'S BRAIN TUMOR nightmare was such a grueling experience, filled with hope, disappointment, fear, and exhaustion. I would have never been able to get through any of it without my mom and mother-in-law. Both lived out of state, but they took turns coming to Chicago and staying at our house, taking care of the kids so I could get to the hospital each day.

Our friends were so wonderful about driving our kids to their classes and taking them to their houses to play. I was really trying to keep the kids' lives as normal as possible—as normal as things could be with Daddy not home and Mommy gone all day.

Kids like "routine"; they like knowing what to expect. Our kids' routine was blown out of the water. Our daughter, Alex, slept with Eric's picture under her pillow and fell asleep many nights crying. Thankfully, Tommy was only 10 months old and was oblivious to what was going on.

It's interesting to me that when a person is going through a huge life-altering crisis such as a loved one's illness, you seem to check out of your regular life and live the "go-to-the-hospital-everyday, trying-to-keep-things-together, hanging-by-a-thread" life.

I was able to do the minimum things necessary to avoid further pitfalls. I could go through the mail, pay the bills that were coming due, make sure the kids were clean and fed, either by me or someone else, but I felt as if I wasn't really there. It was as if my mind had a thick steel shell that dulled any human emotions and it allowed me to forge ahead to do what I had to without falling apart.

A machine-like characteristic took over, chug, chug, chugging through each day. Many days, I'd arrive at the hospital and have no recollection of driving the 24 miles to get there. I would talk to many friends and family each day, but it was always to give the latest update on Eric's condition, explain how he seemed and what the doctor had to say. The phone would ring in the evening over and over and I would repeat the day's update to every caller. It was exhausting, especially at the end of a long day, when I was trying to give my kids some attention before they went to bed.

While running errands, I would look at people and think, "How could you just be grocery shopping so calmly? Don't you know my husband had brain surgery and is very, very sick?" But the outside world keeps churning with the hustle and bustle of everyday life, and somehow you fight the daily battles you need to, in order to continue moving ahead.

The majority of Eric's hospital stay was spent in the neurological intensive care unit. The attention and care he received was incredible. On one hand, I would think how wonderful it was that there were several nurses assigned to Eric, but then I realized it wasn't so great because he was sick enough to need that constant attention.

It took me quite a long time to get used to all the equipment and tubes that Eric required. He had big machines that administered his medications and a monitor that displayed vital statistics that the nurses were always watching closely.

It was also hard to get used to Eric's appearance. I remember when my sister-in-law rode with me to the hospital one night. She said she never would have known that the person lying there was Eric if I hadn't led the way to his bed. Eric's face was very swollen, his eye was bruised, and his head was wrapped in gauze. His arms were bruised from all of the needles and IVs. It was very hard for me to get used to seeing my husband lying in a hospital bed like that.

Soon I had my own "hospital routine." I'd arrive about the same time each day. Even the street vendor selling M&Ms at the expressway exit would wave and smile at me like we were old pals, as he passed my car to pedal sweets to the cars behind me. One day he said, "Hi Curly," referring to my very curly hair. How are you today?" That's when I knew I'd been making the drive too long—I had bonded with the street vendor.

At the hospital, I learned a shortcut through a stairwell that got me up to the ICU faster. I'd grab a bite to eat around the same time each day, again using a back stairwell known only to those "in the know." I had a large canvas purse that I deemed my "hospital bag" in which I'd put my newspaper, along with my notebook for my daily notes, a Diet Pepsi, and anything else I figured I needed. *To this day I cannot use that purse anymore.* I'd see the same hospital workers everyday. As we passed in the halls, they would always acknowledge me with a knowing nod as if to say, "Hello again… Still here, huh?"

Besides seeing Eric and talking with him, my major goal everyday was to cross paths with Eric's doctors and get an update. I have always had a huge amount of respect for doctors. Completing the years of school required to be a doctor shows impressive dedication in itself, but the mere fact that they are brave enough and confident enough to take responsibility for other people's lives, performing surgery or prescribing medication is incredible to me.

When someone is smart enough and skilled enough to do something like cut open my husband's skull and perform brain surgery, the "God complex" I attach to them is immeasurable. Each day, as I sat next to Eric, I would watch the activity out in the nurses' station, hoping to catch the doctor's arrival.

This was a teaching hospital, so when our doctor walked the halls, he was surrounded by a group of students wearing white coats. They were like groupies, hanging onto the doctor's every word and busily scratching notes onto their pads as he spoke.

When I would see them coming down the hall, my hope was always for good news. I hoped they were looking for me… the family of the patient that they just discovered the cure for all that ails him and he'd be 100% by tomorrow, completely back to normal and able to come home. *Sure.*

Waiting for the daily doctor sighting was always nerve wracking. I think he's coming. Is that him? Cue the trumpets and harps, roll out the red carpet and turn on the moving search lights… Ladies and gentlemen, please welcome the all knowing, ever powerful, can-do-no-wrong-in-my-book man, whose hands were in my husband's brain, Dr. T.

After my big build up of the doctor's arrival, my interaction with the doctor was frequently a letdown. I could never remember the questions that I was going to "for sure" ask. It was as if someone shook my Etch-A-Sketch brain and POOF! All my "need to know" questions were erased. The doctor always spoke very quickly and seemed to be in such a hurry. He'd look at Eric's chart and ask Eric how he was doing. If we were dealing with an infection or fever, he'd tell me what was being done to try and get things under control, but our conversations always lasted only four to five minutes.

I don't know what I expected. Did I want him to pull up a chair and have a daily chat over some Jell-o? He's a brain surgeon, for God sakes; he probably had a few things going on. Whatever I was thinking, my interactions with Eric's doctor always fell short of my expectations, however unreasonable they might have been. I imagine it was because when I was able to choke out a question, his answer was almost always, "We don't know. Every patient is different and every tumor is different. We'll just have to wait and see."

Wait and see. Not the words someone with absolutely no patience wants to hear. I am the president of the instant gratification club. Wait? No way. When I wanted to do something, I wanted to do it right away. If I had to wait, it was excruciating. Now, with Eric in the hospital, and everyday a new medical challenge, all I could do was wait. How strange it was to have to wait and see how your life would turn out.

Eventually, I grew very accustomed to the hospital life, but every now and then, I'd be struck by something that would shock me into coping with the big picture, like seeing my husband in restraints or realizing, "Oh my God, I'm spoon feeding my 43-year-old husband."

I also dealt with tremendous guilt. On the days I didn't go to the hospital, I could spend time with the kids. At the same time, I felt guilty for not being there for Eric. When I was at the hospital, I felt guilty for being away from the kids. Talk about a lose/lose situation.

The doctor decided he would perform a second surgery just six days after the first to go back in from a different angle and remove as much of the tumor as possible. Over his three-and-a-half-month hospital stay, Eric encountered many complications. Everyday, I was informed of another problem they were trying to get under control. He had fevers that were very difficult to control. They packed him in ice and covered him with cooling blankets.

Eric had a fast heart rate, elevated pressure on the brain and his body could not regulate his fluid input and output, which created dehydration and dangerous sodium levels. He had many infections: a urinary tract infection, several blood infections, an infection that blew his left arm up like a balloon, and a very drug-resistant staph infection, causing them to put Eric in isolation. He also developed pancreatitis and had surgery to have his gallbladder removed. He was on and off the ventilator (a machine that breathes for the patient when they can't breathe for themselves) three times.

This was in the middle of Eric's 3 1/2 month long hospital stay. He was in isolation for a while so I had to wear a gown and gloves.

A parade of doctors consulted on Eric's case during his hospital stay. It was only months later, when the bills started rolling in, that I realized how many doctors saw Eric for his many medical issues.

All the while, Eric was unaware of what had happened to him, where he was, or even what month or year it was. He didn't recognize me as his wife. He thought I was just a friendly nurse. I told him he better not have been kissing all the other nurses like he was kissing me!

Eric would not leave his IVs and tubes alone. He was constantly pulling them out every chance he got, despite many, many orders from me, and the nurses, to leave them alone. Now you see the IV, now you don't. They had to put restraints on Eric's arms to stop him from pulling them out.

Eric's veins were very hard to stick because of the number of times he had been stuck. When he would yank out his tubes, a handful of nurses, one after the other, would try to find a new vein. They once stuck him on the top of his feet just to have a working IV.

Speaking of feet, I want to know what happens to peoples' feet when they go into the hospital. People get ugly, "old people" feet. It's as if being in the hospital has a directly negative effect on the appearance of patients' feet. Besides being gross, in a purely selfish thought, *I am too young to have a husband with "old people" feet.* (I feel better now that I got that off my chest.)

A few things were becoming clear to me about Eric. First, his memory was almost non-existent. He would ask me the same question over and over, with just a few minutes in between. He also didn't remember key facts of his life or recognize family members.

Second, Eric's demeanor was very calm. Too calm. Passive. Too passive. Easy going. Nothing got him riled up or mad. On the plus side, he was very pleasant to all the hospital staff and they liked working with him.

However, as his wife, I felt like the lights were on, but nobody was home. He showed no emotions. I even wondered if he had the ability to feel physical pain. He had two brain surgeries, six days apart, his head was full of staples, and he never once complained of a headache. He had a million needle pokes for IVs and never even winced.

Third, in layman's terms, he was nuts. Crazy. Loopy. Loony. Most everything he said was goofy talk. My apologies to the medical field, but this is the only way I know to describe it. There also appeared to be a word retrieval problem. It was as if Eric knew what he wanted to say, but when he couldn't think of the word he wanted, he substituted it with a made-up word.

Finally, it seemed nothing Eric said was based in reality. Well, my and your reality that is. It appeared Eric had his own reality. He would say things that I knew were completely untrue, but in his mind they were unequivocally true and there was no arguing with him about it.

Looking for a Sign… Or the Boss Trumps the Wife!

I STARTED TAKING NOTES of what happened in the hospital from the start so that when Eric was recovering he could read about what happened to him. *I am glad I took the notes because I never would have remembered everything, but sadly, Eric never recovered enough to understand what he went through.*

February 26 – (One day after his first surgery.)
The nurse asked, "Eric, do you know where you are?"
Eric answered, "St. Claire Hospital."
This is the hospital in Pittsburgh where Eric grew up. We were actually in a Chicago suburb.

February 28 – (Three days after his first surgery.)
Eric called me Denise, the name of his brother's ex-wife. He asked me if his brother said it was okay that I was there.

March 1st – Eric asked Dr. T, his brain surgeon, if he used a power tool for his surgery. The doctor said no, that they used other things and Eric said, "That's good."
Over and over, Eric asked what day it was and what time it was, and if it was day or night, even though there was a window next to his bed and he could easily see out. He repeatedly said he wanted to go home and take a shower and kept trying to get out of bed.
Eric said, "My dad is out there in the hallway walking backwards."
Every few minutes, Eric would say, "Let's get going." Then I'd launch into the whole explanation that he had just had brain surgery four days ago and needed to stay in the hospital to recover. He'd say, "Oh," with a thoughtful look that really made it seem as if he was

thinking about what I just said. Then, a few minutes later he'd say, "Let's get going."

March 2ⁿᵈ – When I was saying goodbye to Eric and leaving the hospital to go home, Eric waved and said, "*Ciao, ciao* for now."

This was a personal sign-off that a local Chicago food critic used at the end of all his TV reports. I wondered if Eric was picking up things from the TV that was on in his room throughout the day.

Eric also asked me if we were going home on the same flight. I told him we drove here.

March 3ʳᵈ – Eric's second surgery was today. The doctor said it was a difficult surgery. There were feelers wrapped around key areas of the brain. Most of the month of March consisted of many medical ups and downs, with the doctors and nurses trying to keep Eric's condition stable.

On March 6ᵗʰ, Eric's parents went to the hospital in the morning because I had been up all night with Alex, who was having bad breathing problems due to her asthma.

The doctors informed his parents that Eric had a bad infection and they were treating him with massive doses of antibiotics. They said that Eric possibly had blood in his stomach and the GI doctors would be involved and, while Eric was the sickest patient in the hospital and getting the most attention, he had the most potential of walking out of there.

I went to the hospital later in the afternoon with our good friend, Rick, and the nurse stopped us from going into Eric's room. She said they were doing an ultrasound to see if Eric was bleeding in his stomach. The nurse said to me, "He's a sick guy, but he's strong."

Rick and I went to the cafeteria and as we were sitting down chatting, Rick noticed someone scanning the crowd and asked me if the person was Eric's doctor. Sure enough it was.

The doctor came to the cafeteria looking for me. *It's never good when they're looking for you.* Dr. T asked if he could speak to me for a while and I told him he could talk in front of Rick. The doctor's line was, "Eric is a sick guy." *Those were also the nurse's exact words. I pictured in my mind a staff alert saying, "Anyone who sees the wife, the party line is that he's a sick guy."*

The doctor said that they were giving Eric blood and that the infection in the spinal fluid was under control, but now, he had a urinary tract infection. He said Eric had blood loss and they were checking to see if it was caused by a stress ulcer. *Maybe I better get checked too because I think all the blood in my face just drained.*

The doctor said he'd like to see Eric's fever and heart rate come down. Then he repeated the words, "Eric is a sick guy, but he's strong."

The doctor then got up, shook Rick's hand, said he'd be in touch, and left the cafeteria.

When I think back to this day, I remember the doctor staring at me so intensely when he said," Eric is a sick guy." He looked at me with the same intensity that he did during our very first appointment, when he was staring at me, explaining Eric's condition, and I had thought he was confused about who had the tumor.

My take on the conversation in the cafeteria was that the doctor was really trying to prepare me for the possibility of Eric not making it. Of course, I realize this in hindsight. At the time, I knew we were struggling through this illness, but I hadn't allowed myself to entertain the possibility of Eric not making it. *At least not out loud.*

March 23rd – The nurse asked Eric if he knew the man standing next to his bed (his dad) and Eric said, "Yes…Guido Sardido."

Again, I wondered if this was influence from the TV being on in his room. Maybe he saw an old Saturday Night Live show rerun with a character named Father Guido Sarducci. Or maybe, when the nurse asked him if he knew the man next to him, his brain thought "father" right away, but when he answered it came out Guido Sardido because the character's name starts with "Father."

Was Eric's crazy talk based on some shred of reality, or something Eric heard and then added to it? *Don't worry, I eventually got over trying to figure this stuff out.*

March 23rd – I told Eric that his dad was with me at the hospital. He looked at his dad and said, "That's not my dad." I told him that it was and he said, "No it's not."

I'm sure that was heartbreaking for his dad. I can relate. So far, I'd been a friendly nurse and his brother's ex-wife!

March 23rd – We taped a bunch of family pictures up on Eric's hospital room wall to make it seem a little more like home. One day, when Eric's cousin, Mary, was visiting, she took the picture down of herself and her two sisters and asked Eric if he recognized each of them. I found this interesting because Eric's three cousins were like sisters to him and I had no doubt he'd recognize them.

First, Mary pointed to her sister, Kathleen, and asked Eric if he knew who she was. Eric said, "No." Then Mary pointed to herself in the picture and asked again. Eric said, "No." Then she pointed to her sister, Barbara, and Eric said, "Yes."

Mary said, "Really? What's her name?"

Eric said, "Vagina."

Mary nearly busted a gut laughing, as I did when she told me the story.

Later, when Mary told Barbara the story, Barbara said that before Eric's surgery, they were chatting on the phone and she told him she had tickets to go see the Vagina Monologues. My God. He must have remembered that, but was unable to sort out the jumbled information in his brain and he called Barbara, Vagina. Don't think Barbara will ever live that down in this family!

March 24th – The doctor suggested that we bring in Eric's favorite music and play it in his room to stimulate his brain. Eric was a huge Bruce Springsteen fan, so I brought some Springsteen CDs, along with some others. As I sat with Eric, listening to the music, he sang along to the song "Thunder Road" and knew all the words. I was really insulted. Eric didn't know me, his own wife, but he remembered all the words to Thunder Road. *Apparently, The Boss trumps The Wife.*

March 24th – Eric's mom and I were visiting and Eric's mom was touching my hair saying to Eric, "Isn't her hair so nice?"

Eric's response was, "It's indescribably soft."

Then Eric pointed to his mom's hair and said, "But what's up with that hair?" We cracked up laughing.

Eric's mom then asked, "What do you think of my hair?"

Eric said, "It's indescribably middlethorp."

What? We had no idea what he was saying. This was our first exposure to Eric making up words.

March 24th – It was clear that since his surgery, Eric's sense of time was all messed up. He didn't believe how long we had been married or even if we were. I told Eric, "It's now the month of March. In July we'll be married 10 years."

Eric said, "No, that's not right." He just seemed so unfamiliar with me. It was like he really didn't know me.

My mom and I were joking, saying that Eric was probably thinking, "Geez, I just met this girl and she's trying to convince me we've been married 10 years."

When I relayed this story to my friend Julie, she said that Eric was probably thinking to himself, "Next she's going to try and tell me we have a couple of kids." We laughed and laughed. I can just imagine him demanding blood tests to prove the kids are his and when I tell him that we adopted the kids, he'd probably think it was part of the whole scam!

On this same day, a physical and occupational therapist came to Eric's room and told me that the goal for the day was for Eric to be able to swing his legs over the edge of the bed and stand up. Up until now, they had worked on range of motion and resistance exercises with his arms and legs, while Eric was lying in bed.

It took quite a while to accomplish the goal and it dawned on me that Eric had to learn this stuff all over again. It also made me realize how much is taken for granted. When the alarm clock goes off and you pop out of bed, that simple task can be so difficult for some people.

Eric had to re-learn that he had to put weight on his hands in order to scoot his butt to the edge of the bed. His legs were huge, very thick and swollen, like tree trunks. You couldn't see his kneecaps, or anklebones. The therapists told me that the swelling was from being in bed for so long and would go down when Eric started to move around.

They tried to bend Eric's legs to put slippers on his feet and that was really painful for him. That same day, Dr. T told us they were thinking of moving Eric to the rehab floor in the next few days.

Notes to Eric — March and April '03

The following are excerpts from my daily notes to Eric, to tell him exactly what happened each day in the hospital.

March 24th – Today Don Guinter visited you. (Eric's good friend.) Don told me he didn't identify himself when he arrived. He said he talked to you about sports and the latest happenings in the steamship industry. Don said when he was leaving that you said, "Bye Don."

March 27th – When I arrived today, they had you sitting in what they called a cardiac chair. It looks like a large lazy boy recliner. It was nice to see you out of your hospital bed.

Today, you stood up with the therapists. They handed you your toothbrush and some toothpaste, but you weren't able to get the paste on the brush. You could move your hand to your mouth and put the brush in your mouth, but it was very shaky. You commented that it had been a long time. Who would ever think you'd have to re-learn putting toothpaste on your toothbrush?

March 28th – You stood up today and took a few steps forward and backward with the therapists. They told you that you did a great job, especially using your hands to push off from the bed. You said to them, "You liked that huh?" Then you flashed them the thumbs-up sign. Here's a hint of your personality/sense of humor coming back. Is it too much to hope for?

Dr. T came into your room today. You introduced yourself to him and Dr. T told you he knew you from long ago in a land far away. He told you he knew you intimately, but not in the biblical sense!

I noticed, while you were doing your therapy, that I could see your ankles and kneecaps. Just a few days ago, your legs were like oak tree trunks. Things are really looking up.

The doctors said they want to do a scope down your throat to look at your pancreas because it is swollen and your blood work shows your liver and pancreatic enzymes are elevated. (*Who knew anything about this stuff?*) They explained it could mean a blockage of some kind. They need to check for blockages because if there are any, a life-threatening infection could develop and you would be very uncomfortable and not feel like eating. I gave them approval for the procedure.

March 29th – Your mom and I walked through the door of the ICU and Dr. T grabbed my elbow and turned us around quickly. He told us he wanted to talk to us outside. (*I knew this couldn't be good.*) He told us you were very sick. He said at 3:00 a.m., you started breathing very heavily. He said it could have been a possible reaction to the scope procedure, but they don't know for sure. They are going to put you back on the vent because you will tire yourself out breathing so heavily.

Your mom and I stayed until the anesthesiologist put you under, then they put the ventilator tube in.

This setback was twice as hard to take because Eric had come so far. He was standing and taking steps and talking a blue streak, even though most of what he said didn't make sense, and now, this. I hated the ventilator, but I guess I was grateful they have it to get patients through the rough spots.

March 30th – We got a call from a doctor on the ICU floor at 9:45 p.m. You pulled out your ventilator tube, but you're doing well. *Ouch.*

March 31st – Dr. T called the house this morning, just as your mom and I were about to leave for the hospital. He said you were doing great.

When we walked into your room you said, "Hi Mom." This is the first time you recognized your mom. Then I asked you if you knew my name and you said, Uhhhhh…Wendy." You were teasing me. Your tone was as if to say, "Duh, like I wouldn't know your name." (*Does a friendly nurse or your brother's ex-wife ring a bell?*)

Your mom and I were so happy. You were very talkative through our whole visit, although the majority of it was crazy talk. We didn't care. You knew us today. Things were looking up.

April 2nd – Jane (my friend from college) and Barbara, (Eric's cousin) came with me to visit you. As we were chatting, you kept asking what time it was and when I asked why you needed to know the time you said that your date was waiting out in the car. I said, "I hope you left the window open a crack because she's been in there for over a month!"

April 3rd – Today is my birthday. You didn't look so good today. Your nurse said you were very congested and they were suctioning out your nose. You couldn't really talk today. Your voice was very faint and breathy.

April 4th – At 12:45 a.m., the phone rang at home and woke me up. (*It's never good news when the phone rings in the middle of the night.*) It was Dr. Z calling from the hospital. He told me they wanted to put a catheter in your head to measure your head pressure. He said you just weren't as responsive and "bright" as you had been. I gave consent. They promised to call if anything happened the rest of the night. I did not get another call that night. *Or anymore sleep.*

April 5th – They informed me that they found some bacteria growing in one of your tubes and they think that was the cause of your lack of responsiveness.

April 5th – You pulled your nose tube out today. Dr. Z says your pancreas and liver enzymes are being watched. You have a severe shake in your hands and arms because your liver can't filter all the toxins.

April 6th – You pulled out another IV. When I walked in your room you were holding a hormone patch in your hand that you took off. *(Eric is managing to pull all these tubes out, even with his arms restrained.)*

April 7th – When I told you "I love you," you said, "One day, you call me a Marlowe and now you're saying this."

I asked, "What's a Marlowe?"

You replied, "I don't know, but I know it's not good."

(Marlowe's was the name of our favorite local restaurant.)

April 7th – While I was visiting you, I put my head down on the bedrail and closed my eyes to rest. You started talking and startled me a bit and I opened my eyes. You said, "Sorry honey. I didn't mean to wake you up."

I was so thrilled with your comment. It seemed so familiar. Like you really knew me and cared for me. It's amazing to me, the little things we hang on to, in order to maintain some hope.

April 9th – You pulled out your picc line today *(your main IV.)*

April 11th – Dr. T's intern told me you would be going to rehab Monday. She advised that you will have your IV in, which is normally against the rules of the rehab floor. She said you still need your IV because your pancreatitis is still an issue. They are making an exception for you.

April 12th – Today is a great day. You walked two laps around the nurses' station pushing your IV pole. You are walking very stably and you are very awake, alert and talkative. There is still a lot of crazy talk, but that is to be expected. You are very affectionate to me. I seem very familiar to you, which makes me so happy.

When I told you I was leaving and I'd see you tomorrow you said, "So I won't be seeing you anymore today?" It seems you are starting to think about time.

April 13th – Dr. S, the general surgeon, *who I think looks like the actor, William Shatner*, told me that tomorrow he would put in a drainage tube, so they could drain the sludge from your gallbladder. He said the tube would remain in for several weeks or until you are strong enough for gallbladder surgery. *Beam me up, Scotty.*

April 14th – When I arrived today, you were sitting up in a chair with the table pulled close. You were using it as a desk, writing a "to do" list. I could not read what you wrote. Your writing was crooked. It seemed like your vision was not good and you couldn't see what you were writing. You were writing words on top of words.

April 15th – They tell me you'll move to the rehab floor today. I see they put in the tube with the drainage bag. The stuff that's draining into the bag is an icky dark green color. Very gross looking.

Today, you asked me if I came from California. I said, "No, our home is in Illinois, only about a 50-minute drive away." I think you thought I was your brother's ex-wife again because she lives in California.

On the Rehab Floor and Looking for Attention... or a Haircut From a Professional?

THE PREPARATIONS TO MOVE ERIC to the rehab floor didn't start out smoothly the morning of April 15th. The nurse had her aide remove Eric's Foley catheter. When she did, Eric screeched in pain and was bleeding quite a bit. (*At least now I knew he had the ability to feel pain.*)

The nurse then informed me they had to put another catheter in to make sure Eric didn't have a tear that would prevent him from urinating. They put another catheter in which was, again, painful for Eric.

Then, we waited around all morning for a wheelchair to show up to transport Eric to the rehab floor.

Arriving on the rehab floor was very scary for me. They dropped us in Eric's room and we didn't see anyone for about an hour. For the whole hour, Eric was trying to pull out his IV, while I was constantly telling him to leave it alone.

All I could think of was how downstairs in ICU he had several nurses looking after him around the clock. Now, here we sat in Eric's fifth floor room all alone, watching the tumbleweed blow down the hallway, with no sign of another existing human life.

A nurse's aide was the first person to show up. I told her Eric had an IV and that he pulled them out frequently. I tried to explain to her about Eric's lack of memory and his crazy talk, but I felt terrible talking about Eric when he was sitting right there. They restrained Eric's hands and it broke my heart.

I started to cry when I told Eric that I had to leave and he said, "You don't have to leave."

I said, "Yes, I do. I have to go home and take care of the kids."
Eric said, "What kids?"
I said, "Ours."

Eric just had a blank look on his face, but didn't say anything. I cried the whole way home.

The rehab floor was really quite impressive. It was actually a very busy floor with lots of people coming and going in all directions. *Where was everyone the day we arrived?* There was a large gym with lots of equipment for physical therapy and occupational therapy, a smaller room used for various therapies, several offices, a front desk and nurses' station and a doctor assigned specifically to the rehab floor.

The patient rooms were very cheerful and spacious, with wide door openings to accommodate wheelchairs. It was a rule on the rehab floor that all patients must use wheelchairs. Each room had its own bathroom, which also was very large with "wheel in" shower access. Every patient room had a dry-erase board and each night their schedule for the following day was written on the board.

All patients were to wear "workout" type clothing and it was amazing what a difference it made not seeing everyone in hospital gowns.

When I arrived the next day, Eric was wearing a t-shirt and shorts. It was so great to see him in real clothes.

His occupational therapist, Carrie, was working with him on sorting colored blocks on a coordinating grid. She told me she had worked with Eric earlier on both getting dressed and brushing his teeth. It was hard for him to get toothpaste on his toothbrush because his depth perception was off. *OK. My 43-year old husband is sorting blocks and can't get toothpaste on his toothbrush. The reality of the situation was starting to sink in.*

When Eric's therapies were done for the day, we were sitting in his room and a nurse came in. She told me Eric was grossly incontinent. *These were her exact words.* He was on IV fluids and liquid nutrition. This did not shock me because for the last month and a half in the ICU, Eric had a catheter, so urinating was never an issue.

Now, here he was in a wheelchair with an IV in his arm and very little attention from the nurses, compared to the attention he received in the ICU. I didn't think Eric had the ability to think, "OK, I have to go to the bathroom. I need to press this nurse button now, so they can come and help me."

I talked to the nurses and tried to work out a system where they asked Eric several times a day if he had to use the bathroom or just brought him in the bathroom several times a day, but they said they were too busy to commit to a regular time each day. *That's comforting.*

On April 17th, Eric had a full schedule, which consisted of two sessions each of occupational therapy (OT), and speech and language therapy (SPL), and one session each of physical therapy (PT) and group OT.

When I told Eric the date and year, he asked, "Did I just sleep through three and a half weeks or something?" I said, "Yes, you did," and explained the whole story, from his symptoms, to his surgery, to his setbacks, and how well he was doing now. I explained to him that he was very sick and on lots of drugs and that he slept a lot and that's why he was losing time in his mind.

During Eric's 11:00 a.m. break, I asked him several times if he needed to use the restroom and each time he said, "No." *No husband of mine will be grossly incontinent.*

At noon, Eric wanted to lie in bed, so I said, "Let's go to the bathroom first, then you can lie in bed." I helped Eric maneuver his wheelchair and his IV pole into his bathroom, which was no easy task. I put the wheelchair brakes on, as I had seen the therapists do in all of his sessions. I finally got Eric standing up, took the brakes off the wheelchair, moved it back and moved the IV pole off to the side so Eric had a clear path to walk to the toilet.

When I turned back around to face Eric, I noticed his legs were trembling, and knew it was just a matter of seconds... he was going down. I only had enough time to reach for Eric and try to steady him. Before I knew it, we were both on the bathroom floor. We didn't really crash to the floor. It was more like a slow tumble. I felt the pressure of all 238 lbs. of Eric against me, as I tried to ease him to the ground. My body acted like a mat to cushion Eric's fall.

There we were, lying in a heap on the cold bathroom floor. From what I could tell, Eric was fine, physically, no injuries from our trip to the floor. So, all I had to do then was get him up and back in his wheelchair. *Yeah, piece of cake.*

I got up and moved the chair just behind where Eric was sitting. Then I moved the IV pole next to the chair. Eric was sitting under the sink and next to the toilet. I first told Eric to grab my hand and I'd pull him up off the floor to a standing position. We tried this, but I was clearly not strong enough and he couldn't brace his legs.

I looked to see what Eric could grab and pull up on, while I pulled his other arm, but the sink was too high and he couldn't scoot into the correct position to push off of the toilet.

I told Eric we needed to pull the emergency chain in the bathroom that automatically called the nurse and he said, "Yeah, that's what we need, more people in this bathroom." I started laughing hysterically and I was thrilled to hear some of Eric's old sense of humor again.

We continued to try different positions to get Eric off the floor, but nothing was working. Approximately 15 minutes passed and I heard a nurse walk into Eric's room. She looked into the bathroom and saw the two of us sitting on the floor and asked very tersely, "What is going on?"

I said, "I was taking Eric to use the bathroom, when his legs started to tremble and he went down."

The nurse didn't respond to me, but leaned her head out of Eric's room and bellowed very loudly down the hall, "I need some help in 5308! The wife thought she could take him to the bathroom."

She yelled this as if I wasn't right there in a heap with my husband on the bathroom floor. I didn't say a word, but I could feel my face burning up with embarrassment.

Within about a minute, two nurses entered Eric's bathroom. One slipped a wide, long belt around Eric's belly and held the strap in her hand. The other grabbed Eric under his right armpit and they counted, "One, two, and three."

They pulled and lifted, and up, off the floor came Eric, as if he were light as a feather. The nurses guided him back into his wheelchair, all the while never acknowledging my presence.

The one nurse thanked the other for her help and wheeled Eric out of the bathroom into his room. She finally made eye contact with me and with a tone of utter disgust asked, "Is there anything else you need?"

I said, "I don't need anything, but Eric needs to use the bathroom." I sat on the bed while the nurse helped him use the restroom. *No husband of mine will be grossly incontinent.*

The nurse manager on the rehab floor informed me that Eric's awareness was only of himself and that he had no short-term memory. He was not sleeping at night, so they were going to keep him awake in the common area until around 10:00 p.m. to see if that would help him sleep better.

The next day, the occupational therapist told me that Eric washed up at the sink and got dressed mostly by himself. It sounded like such a small task, but Eric had been lying in a hospital bed for a month and a half, so everything was a milestone.

Seeing Eric on the rehab floor, restrained in his bed, was very sad. They also had him playing with children's toys to keep his hands busy, so he didn't pull out any more IVs.

On April 18th, my mom and I visited Eric. I was still very nervous about the decrease in attention Eric was getting on the rehab floor, compared to when he was in the ICU. When Eric was not in a therapy session or when therapy was over for the day, there were long periods of time when Eric was alone between nurse visits. He still had no short-term memory, and an IV that he was always attempting to pull out. I had spoken to the nurses many times, but they were very busy and didn't seem able to find the time to address my concerns.

As my mom and I were visiting with Eric, Dr. T, Eric's brain surgeon walked in and checked Eric's chart. I asked him how he thought Eric was doing and he said, "Physically good, but mentally, it will be slow and long."

I told Dr. T that I was planning to bring our three-year old daughter to visit Eric the next day. It would be the first time she had seen her daddy in a month and a half, since kids weren't allowed in the ICU.

Eric's hair looked terrible. His head was shaved in the areas of the incisions from surgery, but the rest of his hair was long and gross. I asked Dr. T if he knew anyone who could shave Eric's head before tomorrow. I thought a shaved head with a baseball hat would be better than his current "do."

Dr. T said he had a few other stops to make, but that he could probably find someone who could help us. Dr. T left and we continued our visit with Eric.

Approximately 45 minutes later, in walked Dr. T again, this time, with a shaver and a sheet. He threw the sheet around Eric and started shaving his head.

The nurse techs and nurses, who had just about ignored us, walked in, and their eyes nearly popped out of their heads! I told Dr. T that I certainly hadn't expected him to be the one who would shave Eric's head.

During the "haircut," the fifth floor doctor walked in and said to Dr. T, "I didn't know you did hair too!"

I said, "You know these brain surgeons, they need a career to fall back on." Dr. T then gave Eric the royal treatment, complete with a head massage and a shirt change.

I know all of the nurses and staff were probably wondering, "Who is this Eric Posey? He must be a good friend of Dr. T."

The haircut story must have gotten around the floor because it seemed to me that Eric was getting much more attention after Dr. T's visit.

Daddy's Got a Boo-Boo on His Head

ON SATURDAY, APRIL 19TH, my mom stayed home with Tommy, while I took Alex to visit Eric for the first time. I had been so nervous about this day because I didn't know how Alex or Eric would react. What I knew for sure was that Alex had been crying herself to sleep because she missed her daddy so much. But how would she react when she finally saw him? Would she be afraid of him?

I had been talking with Alex about Daddy and explained that he had a boo-boo in his head that the doctor had to take out and that was why he was in the hospital. I also told her Daddy wouldn't have any hair on his head, but it wasn't a big deal because hair grows back.

I asked our adoption social worker, Mary, if she would come to the hospital with me and Alex today. Mary was our social worker assigned to us when we adopted both Alex and Tommy and I thought if Alex or Eric reacted badly, maybe she would have a better idea of how to handle it than I would.

We walked into Eric's room and, according to his schedule, he was in speech therapy. Mary stayed with Alex at the end of the hall, while I went into the speech therapy room and took Eric a baseball hat to wear.

I wheeled Eric into the hallway and when Alex saw us, she slowly walked toward us. Eric smiled and said, "Hi Bug."

He remembered her nickname. I was so thrilled. Eric outstretched his arms wanting to pick Alex up, but he didn't have the strength. I put Alex on Eric's lap and she wrapped her arms around his neck and gave him a big hug.

I brought my camera and proceeded to take a bunch of pictures. Eric really seemed to know Alex and seemed very interested in her and what she was doing. He was smiling at her a lot.

Alex said, "I love you Daddy."

"I love you too," Eric said.

I was trying to hide the fact that I was balling my eyes out in the corner. Mary, Alex, and I attended Eric's occupational therapy session with him. The therapist had Alex help by handing beanbags back to Eric after he tossed them into a grid on the floor.

Our visit far exceeded my expectations. I told Alex that we were going home to color Easter eggs in an attempt to make the "goodbye" easier. She kissed Eric goodbye and waved to everyone as we entered the elevator to begin our trip home.

On Easter Sunday, April 20th, the whole family went to brunch at my brother's house and then Alex and I visited Eric around 4:30 p.m. Eric was lying in bed when we arrived and seemed very tired, although he watched Alex scurry busily around his room. Alex told Eric she forgot to bring him the Easter egg she colored for him and he said she could bring it another time.

Alex didn't want to leave, but we were heading for the elevator around 6:00 p.m. Alex cried and sobbed for the first half of our ride home, repeating, "I miss Daddy," over and over. The crying part was hard, but I think it was good for Alex to know that her daddy was in the hospital, getting better.

This was the first day Alex got to visit Eric in the hospital.

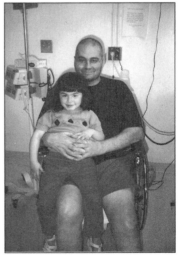

Alex loved visiting Eric in the hospital.

Si Vous Ne Pouvez Pas Rire, Vous Pouvez Aussi Bien Envoyé Dans La Serviette

If You Can't Laugh, You May as Well Throw in the Towel

ON WEDNESDAY, APRIL 23^(RD), Sarah, Eric's speech therapist, told me she was working on some writing exercises with Eric and he was writing in French. It was pretty wild. Eric studied French in college and spent a semester in France, but he had not spoken French in over 20 years.

They were talking about discharging Eric on May 9th. I was freaking out. He still had an IV and still wasn't telling anyone when he had to use the bathroom. How was I going to handle Eric at home under these conditions? We already knew what happened last time I tried to help him to the bathroom. I was picturing myself trying to help Eric up and down the stairs at home with his IV pole and trying to stop Eric from constantly pulling out the IV. How could I handle it? How could I take care of him and two little kids? I felt sick to my stomach. Was this really happening?

During physical therapy, they had Eric walking down the hall and finding plastic blocks that had been put in the corners of the long hallway. This exercise forced the patient to scan far left and right. Eric did this exercise for many days in his usual agreeable, almost hazy state. Then, one day, the therapist asked him to pick up the blocks and Eric said, "There's one," pointing it out and he said, "There's one," pointing to another on the floor.

The therapist asked Eric to pick the blocks up and he said, "No, let's just pretend I did." Eric's comment was dripping with sarcasm. He would not pick the blocks up, which was very unusual for Eric, who was usually so passive and agreeable. This turned out to be the first incident of defiance, but not the last.

In speech therapy, many word exercises were used to determine the level of vocabulary comprehension and the ability to follow a story. Sarah, the speech therapist, read several paragraphs about a man who couldn't get to work on time. The story told how this man set several alarm clocks, even placing one across the room, forcing him to have to get out of bed to turn it off.

Immediately after reading the paragraphs, Sarah asked Eric what the story was about. Eric said, "It was about Ed McMahon's wedding."

What?! I was sitting in the corner observing and after Eric answered, I started laughing at his completely random answer. I was giggling out of control and Sarah, the therapist, began laughing, too. The harder I tried to regain my composure, the harder I laughed, and Sarah struggled to keep it together, too.

It was during this session that Eric called me Debbie Murray. *Whoever the heck that was.* I told Eric my name started with a "W" and then he got my name right. He always needed cues to get to the right answer.

The nurse manager told me that Eric was getting out of all of his restraints. *I'm married to Houdini.* She explained that she had two options. The first option was to find a "watcher" from somewhere in the hospital to sit with Eric, but a "watcher" cannot touch patients, so if Eric pulled out an IV, the watcher couldn't stop him.

The second option was leather restraints. The nurse manager explained that they were responsible for Eric's safety and if he was wandering down the hall, he could be a danger to himself. I told her that I fully understood.

Later, I told my mom that the nurse manager was warning me, so that the next time I walked in and Eric was strapped down like Hannibal Lecter, I couldn't say I wasn't warned!

On April 28th Eric was speaking more French in speech therapy. Sarah, the speech therapist, asked Eric his wife's name and he still needed cues to come up with it. During the course of one visit, Eric would know me in the beginning, forget me in the middle, and know me again at the end. Very strange.

Eric's short-term memory was really messed up. He just couldn't seem to remember as recently as five minutes earlier. On a day when my mom and I were visiting Eric on the rehab floor, Al, a work colleague of Eric's also visited. Eric was just finishing up a session and I said, "Eric, look who is here to visit. It's Al." Eric greeted Al with a handshake and reacted as normally as could be.

We decided that since Eric was done with his sessions, we would go back to his room and visit. Eric wheeled himself down the hall, while my mom, Al, and I, followed.

We sat in Eric's room and chatted with Al, while I fed Eric information, so he'd know what was going on. I said, "Eric wasn't that nice of Al to come and visit you?" Eric usually answered with only one or two words. If his answers were any longer, they were very vague.

At one point, my mom excused herself to go to the restroom and when she came back only about four minutes later, Eric excitedly said, "Hi Mom, how are you?" It was clear to everyone that Eric thought he was seeing my Mom for the first time that day, never mind the fact that we had been with him for the past four hours.

My mom replied politely and told Eric she was fine, but then my eyes met hers and we started giggling. We just couldn't help it. Maybe it was stress, or exhaustion, or both, but someone could have had a gun to our heads and told us to stop laughing and we wouldn't have been able to.

Poor Al. He was just doing a good deed and visiting his friend in the hospital and had to deal with us—the two giggling nut cases. Looking back, laughter helped me through so much of this ordeal. If you can't laugh, you may as well throw in the towel.

More notes...

ON APRIL 29TH, I ASKED the therapists to schedule Eric's physical therapy earlier in the day so I could watch, and I was amazed at what I saw. I had no idea what Eric was capable of, physically. He was walking fairly steadily and was able to walk upstairs using only one handrail. I was thrilled.

In the next few days, Eric's occupational therapist was having him walk down the hall and scan the walls for letters and numbers she had posted on the walls. Eric did well. His parents arrived today and he recognized them both, stood up, out of his wheelchair, and hugged them.

Not so fast. On May 1st, I got a call at 7:15am from the nurse on the rehab floor. She told me Eric's face was flushed and he seemed uncomfortable. When they rolled him over, he was really struggling to breath. They sent him back to the ICU.

Five minutes after I hung up with the rehab floor nurse, a nurse from the ICU called. She told me when Eric arrived in the ICU, he was tachycardic (meaning he had an excessively fast heart rate), his pressure dropped and they did an emergency intubation (put in a breathing tube).

When I arrived at the hospital, a nurse was straightening out all of Eric's tubes. I counted eight towers of medications attached to the IV. It turned out Eric had a blood infection, which caused this latest setback. *Did I have the strength to handle another setback?* Eric was just walking the halls and climbing stairs and now he was back in the ICU. *Yuck.*

A week later, they moved Eric from the Neuro-ICU to the fourth floor ICU, where there were more abdominal patients. According to Dr. T, Eric's brain was no longer an issue. The current concern was all of the infections and gallbladder issues. We were awaiting gallbladder surgery, which finally took place on May 8th and went well.

The doctor was still concerned about Eric's enzyme levels, which I thought would be a non-issue once his gallbladder was removed. Not so. Eric got to feast on clear liquids for a few days while his enzymes were monitored.

Being on a new hospital floor meant dealing with new nurses who didn't know Eric or his antics. As usual, I tried to warn them, but they didn't seem to be interested in hearing my insight. It only took one day and one yanked out IV for the nurses to finally get a feel for the situation.

One day, I walked into Eric's hospital room on the fourth floor and there was a pile of towels and washcloths on Eric's bed. The nurse was having Eric fold towels to keep his hands busy and take his mind off of the IV. We also brought him some puzzles to pass the time and distract him.

Every two minutes, Eric would still ask me where his clothes were and say that he had to get dressed. I would explain that I took his clothes home and would bring them back when he got back to the rehab floor. Almost immediately, he would ask about his clothes again. *Ahhhh.* Eric's short-term memory was shot.

Two weeks after arriving on the fourth floor ICU, Eric was moved again to the fifth floor rehab facility. His first night back, Eric got a fever. *For the love of God!* They took out his picc line, put a new IV in his right hand, and treated him with antibiotics.

For Mother's Day I tried to have Eric write a card for his mom, but he wrote words on top of words, in the shape of a hill and couldn't write in a straight line. He had a very hard time.

There were a lot of issues with Eric's fluid level balance, causing his hands and ankles to be very swollen. Any actions he tried to initiate were delayed. He was unable to stand up from his wheelchair. He stared off into space with a blank look on his face.

When I would say, "Eric, we are going to stand up," he'd say, "Ok," but didn't put his hands on the wheelchair armrests or make any movement at all. It was as if he were frozen and it scared me. I had to pull him up at the armpit, with a lot of force, to get him to stand.

Soon they got his fluid levels balanced and for the first time in three and a half months, Eric wasn't connected to an IV. He was attending all of his therapy sessions and I was told they would discharge him the next week. *Oh my God. Eric was coming home! I could hardly believe it.*

There were many times since his first brain surgery that I didn't think Eric would make it out of the hospital. Now, he had endured two brain surgeries, many blood infections, gallbladder removal, pulmonary embolism, three intubations, countless needle sticks, re-learned basic motor skills and activities of daily living and now he was coming home.

I had so many emotions running through my head. I was grateful Eric survived, but scared out of my mind about whether I could handle taking care of him and our two kids. I was nervous about the unknown future in front of us. How would Eric be at home? Would he get along with the kids? How would the kids react to him? Would he have to re-learn where everything was? Would I have to watch him like a hawk so he didn't wander off?

Was Eric going to be able to walk up the stairs to go to bed at night or did I need to set up our first floor office as a bedroom? If I did, I would have to sleep downstairs as well because I'd be worried Eric might just walk out the front door and wander off. Would I have to deal with his incontinence? *Not the thing at the top of my "can't wait to do" list.* I was thankful Eric no longer had an IV, at least, because I didn't know how I would handle that at home.

I had all these worries and no answers. "Everyone is different" was the line I had been getting from every doctor since we arrived at the hospital, and it was the same line they were giving me as we left to go home. We were going home. *Yikes!*

PART TWO

Back Home, It's a Whole New World

Eric Comes Home - June 4th, 2003

I WAS SO NERVOUS about getting Eric home. The day he was released from the hospital, I asked my brother, Butch, to drive. Most of my stress was from not knowing how Eric would behave. I pictured us driving home and Eric opening the car door to get out while we were speeding down the expressway. With my brother driving us home, I was able to sit in the back seat with Eric, just in case anything happened. Fortunately, Eric slept most of the way home.

I needed to stop at the pharmacy to drop off the pile of prescriptions for Eric. *The first trip of hundreds to come.* While I was in the drugstore, Eric woke up and said to Butch, "This looks like the shopping center at Euclid and Quentin Roads."

Butch said, "It is."

I was nervous all day, wondering how Eric would be once he finally got into the house, and how he would behave with the kids. Now, the time had arrived. Eric was walking through the front door of our home on June 4th, 2003, three and a half months after leaving the house for brain surgery.

When we walked through the door, we were greeted by my mom and our kids, Alex and Tommy. Eric gave everyone hugs and kisses and then went right into the kitchen to pour himself a drink. If you've ever been in someone's house for the first time and you go to find a cup, you usually end up opening several cabinets before you find the right one. Eric opened the right cabinet the first time, grabbed a glass, opened the fridge, and poured himself some lemonade.

The office in our home is located directly across from our first floor powder room. After Eric used the bathroom, he walked in the hallway, reached around the office wall and turned the office light off, the one that I had left on earlier. He knew the light switch was there around the corner. I was amazed and very happy.

He went into the family room, sat in his favorite chair, and started searching through the newspaper basket for the sports page. It seemed by his actions that nothing was different. It was as if the three-

and-a-half month-long brain tumor nightmare had never happened. I turned on the TV and took comfort in the fact that Eric resumed his familiar love affair with the remote control, as he had his entire adult life. There he was, sitting in his chair, repeatedly changing channels, as if today were just another ordinary day.

It would soon become clear that our days would be anything but ordinary. After the "crisis" mode and daily drives to the hospital, after thinking through all the horrible "what if" scenarios, after the "life and death" portion of Eric's illness was over and he came home, that was when the real challenges began.

Personality Shift / Where's the Guy I Married?

BY FAR, THE HARDEST PART of the whole brain tumor nightmare was the change in Eric's personality. There was Eric before surgery and Eric after surgery. I really tried to break the habit of talking about Eric in the past tense. Eric didn't die. He was with me, living and breathing. Except, in a way, he did die because his personality changed so dramatically that he was a completely different person. He was not the man I married and the sad, cruel, brutally honest truth was: if given the choice, I would not have married the "new" Eric.

The "Old" Eric

The "old" Eric was one of the smartest people I ever knew. He knew a lot about many different subjects. You'd never want to play "Trivial Pursuit" against him, and watching "Jeopardy" with him just made you feel dumb. He was an avid reader. He read everything he could get his hands on. It would take forever to get through a museum with Eric because he would read every plaque in the place.

He was a huge sports fan, having played high school and college football, and he was a die-hard Pittsburgh Steelers fan. Eric was addicted to ESPN's Sports Center. He'd watch it three times a night. I felt like the Sports Center anchors, Keith Olberman and Dan Patrick were part of our family.

Eric was very social and a great listener. He could talk to anyone at any level and was genuinely interested in learning about people and their lives. We would go to a party together and not see each other most of the night. He would walk around and mingle, introduce himself and by the end of the night, he'd know everyone. That was a trait I always loved in Eric. He didn't cling to me at parties; he didn't need to be by my side every moment.

He made me laugh. Eric frequently used self-deprecating humor, which always made others laugh. His temperament was very even

Our wedding day. Don't you just love Eric's giant glasses!

keeled. He was easy going, pleasant, and considerate. It took a lot to make him mad.

Now don't get me wrong. There were plenty of things that Eric did that annoyed me. After all, we were a typical married couple. Grape Nuts comes to mind. They were his favorite cereal. I think they are like eating tiny pebbles, but hey, that's just me.

When Eric chewed his Grape Nuts, the loud crunching and slurping were like nails on a chalkboard for me. So many times, I'd offer to cook him eggs for breakfast (the incredible edible—and silent—egg) and he'd say, "I think I'll just grab a bowl of cereal."

Grrrr. It got to where I just went in the other room until he finished, but if, after seventeen years, this is what was at the top of my list, then I think we did just fine.

Eric was <u>always</u> the voice of reason. He liked to have a plan and know what we were going to do each day. I would always tell him he needed to be a little more spontaneous. Surprise! An unexpected brain tumor, that's going to rock your world. How's that for spontaneity? *Be careful what you wish for.*

Welcome Home Mr. Clean

If Eric was aware of anyone else during his early days back home, he would have felt like a lab rat. I watched his every move with nervous intensity. I was nervous he'd fall down, nervous he'd wander off, nervous he'd hurt himself, nervous about everything. I was also trying to figure out what he remembered and what seemed familiar to him.

Once Eric was home, my mom proposed an idea that she and my mother-in-law, Maggie, alternate three-month shifts and stay with us in Chicago to help me get through the first year. Maggie agreed.

My mom took the first shift and boy, was I glad to have her with me. Eric's first day home was emotionally exhausting. I was thrilled that he was home, but the uncertainty of the situation wiped me out. When it was bedtime on his first night home, Eric thought he was supposed to sleep in our guest room. Strange. I finally convinced him that the master bedroom was ours by showing him his clothes in the dresser drawers and closet.

It was a rough first night. Eric woke up every hour to go to the bathroom. Each time he came from the bathroom, he would leave our bedroom and walk down the hall to one of the other bedrooms. Every hour, I had to re-convince him that he belonged in our room. When I would insist that yes, in fact, he was sleeping in the room with me, he would say, "Well, I wasn't sleeping in here, but if you want me to, then ok." *Don't do me any favors.*

Another time he asked me, "Does my brother know about this?" He must have thought I was his sister-in-law again. *Ugh.* I was exhausted, sleep deprived. I felt like I had a newborn baby.

Also, he would lie down on his back, go to sleep with his arms crossed, and not move a muscle all night long. He'd wake up in the exact same position as he had started eight hours earlier. Bizarre. Very vampire-like. I remember many times hovering over him in bed, practically nose to nose with him, checking to see if he was still breathing.

The next few days we didn't do much. We hung around the house and had lots of visitors come to welcome Eric home. Eric greeted his visitors warmly, but then really didn't interact much. Mostly, I spoke for Eric, telling everyone what we had been doing and how Eric was adjusting.

Eric frequently dozed off in his chair during the day. It surprised me how he could sleep through the noise and chaos of a three-year old and a one-year old. The next few nights weren't as bad as the first. He didn't wake up every hour, only about three to four times each night, always attempting to leave our bedroom.

I thought it would be great for Eric to call his parents, his best friend, Eric S., and his friend D.R. in Pittsburgh. I dialed the phone and told him he was calling D.R. As I expected, D.R. was blown away to hear from Eric. I could tell from my end that Eric was answering D.R.'s questions. "Yes, it's nice being home." "The kids are in the yard playing." "I'm feeling pretty good." All the usual answers to the usual questions someone would ask after you return home from a long hospital stay.

Then I heard Eric say, "The reason I'm calling is because I believe you have a pair of ankle weights that belong to me. They're in the front of your garage, so can you check to make sure you have them and let me know?"

WHAT? I had no idea what Eric was talking about and neither did D.R. There were no ankle weights. Eric was talking total nonsense. This was our first experience with Eric's "crazy talk" since he had arrived home, but certainly not our last.

We had a few visitors on Sunday and the rest of the weekend was relatively uneventful. Sunday night, the phone rang and I was busy with one of the kids. I heard Eric talking and before I was able to get to the phone, Eric had hung up. When I asked him who it was, he said, "Vince and his wife."

That's great, except we don't know anyone named Vince...or his wife! I dialed *69 to call back the caller and found out it was my nephew Rick and his wife Michelle. This was the first of many similar incidents that resulted in the addition of caller ID to our phone plan.

Eric was very despondent when he first came home. His affect was flat. Technically speaking, it was as if "nobody was home." He was very passive and had very little interaction with the kids.

Eric never knew what day of the week it was. He didn't even know the month or season, and didn't take any cues from what he saw out the window.

During the day, he sat like a lump in his chair and just observed. If the TV was on, he'd stare at it or just constantly change the channels. He would speak when spoken to, but that was it.

When people converse, they refer to an event in the news or something that someone just said. Eric couldn't remember anything and didn't know what to say, so he didn't start conversations and didn't participate much since he couldn't remember what had already been said.

He would often repeat what someone said or react to what people said with very vague statements. He would say, "That's very interesting," or "Is that right?" If you asked him something specific like, "Do you remember being up at Sand Lake last winter?" he would say, "Yes, it was cold." He really didn't remember anything about being at Sand Lake, but he knew winter was cold, so that is how he responded.

Eric was very smart and I'm sure he thought these vague responses made it appear as if he could remember whatever people were referring to in their conversations. All the years Eric spent as a salesman must have helped him in these situations. He always had an answer, but he almost never initiated any conversation.

As the early days went by, I was getting more used to giving Eric all his medications. There were about nine different pills he had to take because his brain could not produce the chemicals that his body needed. He took anti-seizure medication, thyroid pills, blood thinners, antibiotics, nasal sprays to regulate his fluid levels, pills to help with dementia, cholesterol medicine and hormones. He took some in the morning and some at night, including an injection I had to give him every two weeks. I felt like Nurse Ratched from "One Flew Over the Cuckoo's Nest."

Eric's morning routine was a challenge due to his memory deficit. He would take a shower, then shave. Eric had always shaved with a blade, but now he was taking blood thinner medication so I had to buy him an electric shaver to avoid any cuts.

At first, Eric would start to put shaving cream on his face and begin shaving with a blade, then, when I realized it, I would make him rinse his face and shave with the electric shaver. *Eventually I hid the cream and razor blades.*

Next, Eric would brush his teeth and get dressed. He always had pretty good taste in clothes and could put outfits together. Not anymore. Because he had no idea what month it was, he would pick clothes that, not only, didn't go together, but were for the wrong season. He would put on a heavy hooded sweatshirt and a pair of jeans in June. When

I would point it out to him, he still had a hard time remembering or picking out clothes appropriate for the current weather.

From that point on, I started laying out Eric's clothes every day. I also put a calendar in our room and marked off each day as it passed and tried to train Eric to look at the calendar before getting dressed each morning.

After he got dressed, Eric would go back into the bathroom and start to shave again. I would stop him as soon as I realized he was doing it, but he never believed me that he had already shaved, not even after I would have him feel his face and look in the mirror. It was a constant fight.

He'd eventually give in, load up his toothbrush and start to brush his teeth again. I would tell him that he just got done brushing his teeth a few minutes ago, but he wouldn't believe me. *Yes, ladies and gentlemen, that's my husband, the one with the raw face and bleeding gums.*

When we finally did make it downstairs, many times, I would lose track of Eric while I was doing the laundry or other household chores. I would soon hear the shower running upstairs, and sure enough, Eric was taking another shower. This could be as soon as 15 minutes after we had gone downstairs from showering the first time. This routine went on all day long, day after day. I'd leave Eric in his chair reading the paper, and go in the office to do some paperwork. Then I would hear the water running upstairs and find Eric showering, yet again. All Eric needed was a baldhead and an earring... *I'm married to Mr. Clean!*

I knew I needed some kind of checklist where we could check off each morning task, so Eric could keep track of what he had already done. I typed a list: shower, shave, dress, brush teeth, and made little boxes next to each task.

One morning, I introduced the list to Eric, explaining that because of his memory problem he repeated his morning tasks and that this checklist would help him know what he had done and what he still needed to do. The first checklist morning, after Eric got out of the shower, I reminded him of the checklist and told him to put an "x" in the box marked "shower" so he'd know that he already showered.

Eric, of course, thought this was ridiculous and said, "I'll remember that I showered." I told him that I knew he thought that now, but very soon he'd forget and he'd go to shower again.

In a very disgusted sigh, Eric checked the "shower" box and then he started to shave. When he was done, I asked him to check the box marked "shave" so he would remember that he had already shaved. Again he protested, but ultimately gave in and checked the "shave" box. The same happened after Eric got dressed and brushed his teeth.

We went downstairs and I was feeling particularly proud of myself and my list. *Who doesn't love a good list, anyway?* We had breakfast and slipped into our new routine of Eric reading the morning paper and me doing whatever needed to be done.

Then, sure enough, about one hour after we completed "the list," I heard the darn shower running. I ran upstairs to catch Eric before he got in, but it was too late. He was in mid-shower. When he got out, I explained to him that he just took a shower not one hour earlier and he said, "No, I didn't."

I said, "Yes you did. Do you remember we made a list and you checked off all your items as you completed them?"

I showed him the list with the checked boxes and he said, "I didn't check those boxes."

I said, "Yes, you did."

And with a tone so confident that he almost made me second guess myself, he said, "No, I didn't."

I was about to blow a gasket. At this point, I didn't care if he lived in the damn shower and his skin dried up, cracked off and he shriveled up and disappeared down the shower drain. *OK, not my proudest moment.*

Eventually, I got my composure back and revised the checklist for the next morning. Instead of checking the box, I made a line next to each task and made Eric sign his name on the lines. He still repeated tasks for a long time, but he didn't argue about who signed his name.

This routine lasted several months, but eventually we no longer needed the checklist and he no longer repeated his morning tasks. I felt hopeful that although it took a long time to resolve the issue, with plenty of repetition, it showed that Eric had the ability to learn new things.

Eric was confused about the number of kids we had, and their ages. He could never get them right. Sometimes he was looking for a third child we didn't have. He would ask Alex if she needed her diaper changed, but she was already potty trained. I could have understood if she were in diapers before Eric had his surgery but she wasn't. He would also look for pets we never had. When I would ask what the pet names were, he would say the names of the pets he had as a kid.

Since he had arrived home, Eric made up things constantly. He was always talking about plans we had or places we went that never happened. The interesting part about this was when he talked about these things, he was absolutely sure they were true.

Eric always had bad eyesight and wore glasses most of his life, but the brain tumor had been on his optic nerve and Eric's vision was even worse after surgery. His lack of vision was a constant source of frustration for him—a terrible problem, especially for someone who loved to read. I bought Eric many different types of magnifying glasses and book lights to try to help him see better. It was hard to watch my husband struggle and just as hard to watch the mental deterioration.

Each time we would get in the car, Eric would always go to sit in the driver's seat. I would tell him that he was unable to drive because of the surgery, and he would get up and move to the front passenger seat. I always felt badly telling him he couldn't drive, but he was very passive about it. That would change.

The Doctor Will See You All, Right Now

FAMILY AND FRIENDS SAID they could see subtle improvements in Eric. I could not. I guess I was too close to the situation. I hoped they were right.

Eric's passive behavior and storytelling continued, even when we went to his many doctor appointments. Trips to take Eric to the doctor were like military maneuvers. I would pack up both kids and Eric in the car to drive to the appointment.

When they called Eric's name I would usher along the three of them, following the nurse like a conga line. Then I'd squeeze everyone into the small exam room, along with the Hot Wheels, coloring books, crayons and the obligatory Ziploc bags of goldfish.

I had to go in the room with Eric because the doctors and nurses would ask questions and Eric couldn't give any valid answers. In fact, he would answer their questions with crazy facts that were totally made up, although Eric thought they were true. Each doctor would eventually learn to direct the questions to me. It was very awkward to talk about Eric when he was sitting right there in the room.

Rest In Peace Bob Hope

AT THE END OF JULY, Eric had been home almost two months and one thing was crystal clear, his short-term memory wasn't any better. He couldn't remember if he ate dinner, if he had showered, where we were going, or where we had been. The number of times I answered the same question in just two months was mind-boggling.

One story about his very bad memory, although it wasn't funny at the time, seems to get funnier as the years go by. Like any typical morning at our house those days, Eric was sitting at the bar, reading the newspaper with the radio on. It came over the radio that Bob Hope had passed away at the age of one hundred.

Eric said to me, "Wendy! Did you hear that? Bob Hope died."

I said, "Yes Eric I heard that." About thirty minutes later they were doing a news update on the radio and they announced that Bob Hope had died. Eric said to me, "Hey Wendy did you hear? Bob Hope passed away."

I said, "Yes, Eric, I heard."

In the afternoon, we were watching TV together and during a news update they announced that legend Bob Hope had passed away at the age of one hundred. Eric turned to me and said, "Bob Hope died, can you believe that?"

And I said, with a tight jaw, "Yes, Eric, I can believe it."

He had no memory of all the updates we had already heard. This went on the rest of the day. Every half hour, whether it was on the radio or on TV, Eric would relay the news to me as if it were the first time he had heard it.

By nine o'clock at night, I had enough. The opening story on the news was the death of Bob Hope. This time, when Eric said to me, "Wendy, did you hear that? Bob Hope died," in a very aggravated tone I replied, "Yes. I heard that Bob Hope died."

Then Eric asked a question that pushed me right over the edge... "I wonder what he died of?"

And that was it. I couldn't take it anymore. It was the straw that broke the camel's back. I screamed at the top of my lungs, "HE WAS ONE HUNDRED YEARS OLD, WHAT DO YOU THINK HE DIED OF?!" *Apparently I was out of patience for the day. Gulp.*

Call from An Angel

NOT LONG AFTER ERIC CAME HOME, I got a call from his boss, John. He said that Eric was covered under long-term disability insurance and that he would fill out all the necessary paperwork and send it to me. Can you believe it? How kind of him to inform me of the disability coverage and expedite it on his end. The poor man had to cover a claim for an employee who had only been working for his company for three months. I'm sure his premium cost went up. I don't think he will ever know how much that call and that insurance meant to my family and me.

Hilton Head, Here We Come!

IN SEPTEMBER 2003, three months after Eric had arrived home from the hospital, we flew to Hilton Head Island, SC, where Eric's parents lived. I was nervous about traveling because, not only did I have two small kids (Alex was three and a half and Tommy was one and a half), but I was unsure how Eric would handle traveling. The irony was that Eric had traveled all over the world during his career.

I packed for everyone the night before we left and put the bags by the front door, ready to load into the taxi the next morning. I could have been mistaken for a pharmaceutical sales rep because of the giant bag of medication I traveled with for Eric. We had an early wake up call. I told Eric that we were flying to South Carolina to visit his parents and the cab would arrive in one hour.

He said, "Well, that's the first I've heard of this trip." Of course it was not the first he had heard of the trip. We had been talking about it for months and the kids were very excited.

I "threw" some breakfast into everyone, got them dressed, and the cab arrived to take us to the airport. As we loaded the bags, Eric was sure he left his sunglasses in the house. I told him they were in the carry-on bag, but he insisted and went back into the house. I reached in the bag, got his sunglasses, and showed them to him when he came back out.

I was buckling the two car seats into the cab and Eric patted himself down, unable to find his keys. I told him he didn't need them because I had mine, but again, he insisted and headed back into the house.

Eric came back out to the cab and said he didn't know where the suitcases were. I told him they were already loaded into the trunk of the cab and he asked the driver to open the trunk again because he couldn't find his sunglasses. I explained again that they were in our carry on bag in the cab and I got his sunglasses out and handed them to him. I figured I would let him carry them.

We finally loaded into the cab, Eric in the front seat next to the driver and me in the back between the two car seats. We were off. The kids were quiet, not fully awake, and Eric asked me if I had the plane tickets. I said, "Yes." Then he asked me what airline we were flying and I told him "American."

Every two to three minutes during the cab ride to the airport, Eric patted himself down. First he checked for his wallet, then he checked for his sunglasses, then his keys. He asked me if I had the plane tickets. I told him, "yes." He asked what airline we were flying and I told him, "American." This routine continued for the full twenty-five minute drive from our house to the airport.

With all of the equipment and bags, getting out of the cab felt like another of my morning military maneuvers. While Eric helped the cab driver unload the suitcases out of the trunk, I unhooked Alex's car seat and put it at the curb of the airport, then I unhooked Tommy's car seat and carried him to the curb, then loaded him into the stroller, while holding Alex's hand at the same time. Eric, of course, did one more check in the backseat of the cab to see if he could find his sunglasses. I reminded him they were in his pocket.

I paid the cab driver for the ride, and before I was able to turn around, the cab driver, who had been silent during our entire ride to the airport, touched my arm and said to me, "You have your hands full. I wish you good luck."

His sincerity took me by surprise and I found an instant lump in my throat. When I looked into the eyes of the cab driver, you could almost see the empathy he was feeling for me. I thought it was interesting that in a twenty-five minute cab ride, he seemed to really understand what I was experiencing.

Going through security was the next challenge. The kids and I made it through the metal detector, but Eric did not. Security guards sent him back to the other side to empty all his pockets. What did he have in his pockets? You guessed it. His sunglasses and his keys. He must have appeared suspicious because the security guards pulled Eric aside to do a full check on him.

I could tell Eric was confused, but I kept telling him they check people at random, so just let them check you with the wand, and then we will be on our way. Thank goodness, that is exactly what happened.

We sat in the gate area waiting to board our plane. Of course, when one person in the family had to go to the bathroom, we all had to go because I was too afraid that Eric wouldn't know how to make his way back to the correct gate. We all used the restroom, came back out, and boarded our plane.

On the plane, Eric and I both had aisle seats directly across from each other and the kids were next to me. I was loaded up with snacks for the kids, a newspaper for Eric, and a magazine for myself.

Just about every five minutes, Eric would ask where we were going. He was clever about it. He asked in every different way he could think of. He'd say, "Where is this plane destined?"

A few minutes later he'd ask, "Where are we landing?"

Then he'd ask, "What state are we going to?"

I guess he figured if he changed the question, it wouldn't be like repeating the same thing over and over. I found it interesting that he could remember that he kept asking about the same thing and was aware enough to change his phrasing. I kept telling him we were going to Hilton Head to visit his parents.

I knew it was just a matter of time, and finally, the guy sitting in front of Eric turned around and looked at him. I'm sure he needed to get a look at the guy who kept asking where he was going. Who could blame him? It must have seemed bizarre.

As a parent, when you fly with two little kids and start walking down the aisle, you know everybody on the plane is thinking, "Please God, not me. Don't let them sit next to me." You can practically hear the sighs of relief as you pass each row.

I'm sure they are picturing kids who cry or make a lot of noise or kick the seats. Little did they know that the kids would be fine, but Eric would be the one who might drive them nuts!

When the flight attendant made the announcement over the loud speaker that everybody needed to fasten their seatbelts in preparation for the landing, Eric looked over at me and said, "Where are we going anyway?" I half expected the man who was sitting in front of Eric to turn around and scream at him, "YOU'RE GOING TO VISIT YOUR PARENTS IN HILTON HEAD!" But he didn't, which was nice.

Given the chance, this guy might have swapped for a kid kicking his seat. I told Eric where we were going. I was more than ready to finally get there. Needless to say, it had been a long trip.

Happy to See Me

IN THE FALL OF 2003, we went out for pizza with our group of golf friends to celebrate Eric's birthday. I drove myself, Eric, and another couple in our car. Two other couples drove separately and met us at the restaurant. When we arrived, we all got drinks and stood in the bar area, waiting for our table. I excused myself and went to the restroom. When I returned to the group, Eric looked at me with a big smile on his face and said, "Hi, how are you? What are you doing here?"

I said, "Honey, we came together. I just went to the bathroom." He was quiet and looked confused. *At least he was happy to see me!*

A Very Good Friend

WE GOT INTO A ROUTINE where first thing in the morning, after showers and breakfast, Eric would sit at our bar and read the newspaper. Because his memory was so bad, after he was done with one or two paragraphs, he would forget what he read and read it again. I remember two funny stories about Eric reading the paper.

Our friend, Don, was an absolute angel to Eric and me during Eric's entire illness. After Eric came home from the hospital, Don would pick up Eric and take him to a bar to watch sports on TV, or take him to hit some golf balls at the driving range. He took him to Cubs' games and Bulls' basketball games.

Even though I lived with Eric's memory deficit twenty-four hours a day, seven days a week, his inability to remember big events or things that just happened always amazed me. Going downtown to a Bulls' game is an activity that takes a good part of the night and makes quite an impression. First, there's the drive downtown. Then you sometimes have dinner, which Eric and Don did. Then you watch the basketball game, which is a very stimulating experience. The team is playing, the music plays, there is half-time entertainment, and a loud, excited crowd. Don took Eric to the game and brought him home.

The next morning, Eric was reading the paper and looked up at me and said, "Oh, I see the Bulls won last night."

I said, "YOU WERE THERE!" *I obviously didn't start the day with much patience.*

The other funny story occurred in November or December the year he came home. Eric looked up from reading the paper with the most confused look on his face. I asked him what was wrong and he said, "Is Arnold Schwarzenegger the Governor of California?"

I'm telling you I almost wet my pants laughing. Can you imagine coming out of the hospital after three and a half months and realizing that the Terminator is the Governor of California?

A Very Quick Doctor

IT WASN'T LONG AFTER ERIC came home that I found myself drowning in paperwork. Everyday more envelopes arrived in the mail. Forms from social security, disability, hospital bills, doctor bills, lab bills, insurance forms, explanations of benefits. It was overwhelming. As if I wasn't under enough stress, I worried constantly that something was falling through the cracks. When I wasn't looking through the mounds of paperwork, I was taking Eric to a doctor appointment or to a lab to get blood drawn. *I didn't like this new life.*

One of the letters I received was from the Department of Human Services for Disability Determination. The letter explained that in order for them to make the best possible decision on whether to approve our disability claim, they needed an additional examination by a doctor they appointed, to, and I quote, "evaluate your alleged impairment."

The letter went on to explain that failure to keep the appointment without notifying them could result in a decision that you are not disabled. Finally, they said to be prepared for the appointment to last from 60 to 90 minutes, depending on the level of evaluation necessary. I immediately called the number on the form and made the appointment.

The day of the appointment, I arranged for someone to watch the kids and arrived at the medical center with Eric. I had an armful of magazines to read while I waited. An Asian man came out of the office door, introduced himself as the doctor who would be performing the evaluation and then led Eric into the office and shut the door.

Twelve minutes later, the door opened and out came Eric and the doctor. The doctor told me they were done and he would complete the necessary forms and send them into the state agency. Twelve minutes! I wish I could have been a fly on the wall during that meeting. I can only imagine the things Eric said that assured the doctor that his impairment was valid. I wonder if we broke a record for shortest appointment?

Outpatient Rehab

ONCE ERIC WAS HOME from the hospital, he began attending outpatient rehabilitation. The program closest to our house was about a 30-minute drive one-way and they provided transportation. I went to the initial meetings with Eric and met with some of the personnel and therapists who explained what Eric would be doing in the program.

During one of the meetings, we were sitting at a table and listening to a therapist talk. Eric reached over, grabbed an open can of Coke and guzzled the whole thing down. Before I realized what happened, it was too late. That was not Eric's Coke. We didn't have any drinks. I said, "Eric, no. That's not our drink."

He put the empty can down and said, "I was thirsty."

This really demonstrated Eric's lack of judgment and awareness. He didn't seem to think anything was wrong with drinking someone else's drink.

Eric attended outpatient rehab during July and August. Every morning when I was putting Eric in the car with the driver, Eric constantly patted himself down. He was always looking for something—his keys, hat, or sunglasses. He would search endlessly for these things. The driver was so nice and very patient. He would always tell Eric that he had everything he needed and then told him they needed to go.

In rehab, Eric worked on speech therapy, physical therapy, and occupational therapy. One day, when I was visiting the rehab to watch some of Eric's therapy sessions, they were practicing using the telephone and making calls. Eric called our house and my mom answered the phone. Eric said, "The reason I'm calling is to find out if you are taking care of the U2 navy issue we were discussing."

My mom was so smooth and went right along with it. She said, "When you come home we'll take care of that together."

That was good enough for Eric. He said, "OK, I'll talk to you later," and hung up.

A few days later, we were all sitting outside in front of the house and my mom told Eric that it was so nice to have him home from the hospital. Eric said to my mom, "I wasn't in the hospital. You and I went to mass, had breakfast and went to Russia on that secret mission, remember?" *Who knew my mom and husband were Russian spies? The wife is always the last to know.*

While in outpatient rehab, Eric learned our home address and phone number, where his parents lived, and where my mom lived. These were things he did not know while in the hospital. *Dare I say, progress?*

The Strange, Bizarre and Unexpected...

ERIC'S WEIRD BEHAVIOR, with all the strange stories and bizarre thoughts that he had demonstrated while in the hospital, continued after he came home.

A typical morning went as follows:

5:15 a.m. – I feel Eric roll over in bed to look at the alarm clock. As if on cue, he'd say, "It's 5:15, I better get going."

I'd say, "I have the alarm set for 7:00. We don't have to take Alex to school until 8:45."

Eric would reply, "I have a meeting downtown this morning."

I'd tell him, "No, you don't. We just have to take Alex to school."

He'd reply, "Oh."

Silence again. I'd hear Eric snoring but I couldn't fall back asleep.

5:45 a.m. – Eric would roll over again, look at the clock and say, "I better get going."

I'd tell him, "I have the alarm clock set for 7:00. We have to leave to take Alex to school at 8:45."

Eric would say, "I have to catch a flight to Cleveland this morning."

I'd tell him no, he didn't and explain to him that we just had to take Alex to school.

Silence again until 6:00 a.m. Eric would look at the clock and say, "It's 6:00. I've got to get going."

I'd say, "I have the alarm set for 7:00. We have to leave at 8:45 to take Alex to school.

He'd say, "I have a seminar today."

I'd say, "No, you don't. We just have to take Alex to school at 8:45."

We had some version of this conversation every morning. There was no meeting downtown, no flight to Cleveland and no seminar. But in Eric's mind, he always thought he had to be somewhere. In reality, he wasn't working, nor was he able to work.

When friends or family would call on the phone to talk to Eric, I would only hear his side of the conversations, and you wouldn't believe the tall tales that he would tell. I wish I had half the social life he described to everyone. He would always tell them we had just flown back from some great vacation, or that we had gone to this party or that party the other night. All totally made up. And not only when he was talking on the telephone, we could be anywhere and Eric would start talking about something and sound so convincing, although none of what he was saying was a bit true.

One time, when we were at an eye doctor appointment, the doctor asked Eric how he had been spending his days. Eric said, "Working."

I said, "Well Eric you've been at rehab each day."

Eric replied, "Oh, and rehab," as if he remembered that, but just forgot to say it.

The eye doctor asked him what he did in the course of a day at rehab. Eric said that he did a lot of classroom type things and some physical things such as, and he kind of paused, and then said "Dodge ball."

I just about died. I put my head down and bit the inside of my cheek so that I wouldn't burst out laughing. What a mental picture. A rehab program that's specifically designed for the brain injured and they're playing dodge ball. Somehow I doubt it.

One time, after Eric had blood drawn, we were waiting outside the hospital for the valet to bring our car around and Eric asked me, "Is our flight tonight?"

I looked at him and said, "Our flight where?"

And Eric said, "To Baltimore."

I said, "Why are we going to Baltimore?"

Eric answered, "Because we sold Kipper."

I had never heard the name Kipper in my life. I asked Eric "Who is Kipper?"

Eric answered, "Our horse." *You guessed it… We never had a horse.*

One day, at breakfast, Eric asked me, "What's the name of the guy I'm waiting for?"

I said, "There is no guy. You are going to rehab today."

Eric said, "No, I'm waiting for the guy to come and give me a nose adjustment." *Ug.*

Another weird phase Eric went through was making up that people were trying to hit him or injure him. We were at my brother's house the first Thanksgiving after Eric's surgery. My brother, Eric, and I were sitting on the couch. Eric got up to use the bathroom and said to my brother, "Now I am going to stand up and go use the bathroom, try not to hit me this time." We all looked at each other confused as if to say, "What in the world was he talking about?"

I said, "What, Eric?"

He said that he remembered last time my brother tripped him, and threw him down to the ground. *Where do these thoughts come from? Very strange.*

Eric developed all kinds of strange habits after his surgery. He started dressing in layers for no reason at all. No matter what season it was or what the temperature was outside, he put on two or three t-shirts and two pairs of socks. Even in July.

His eyes also changed after his surgery. They seemed very "buggy," and wide open. And he barely seemed to blink. He would talk at the TV in a sing-songy, high-pitched, very annoying voice, and repeat what he heard on the TV, over and over. He would fill the kitchen sink to almost over-flowing to hand-wash two forks.

Just like a kid, he waited until the last minute to go to the bathroom, doing the adult version of the potty dance. First I'd notice the bouncing foot: heel off the ground, ball of the foot bouncing up and down. Then the leg fanning in and out. Then the frantic crossing of the legs, right over left leg then switch, left over right. It was maddening. When I suggested he go to the bathroom, he'd snap at me, "I WILL! *Arg.*" Very Shrek-like. *Great, I'm married to an ogre.*

Eric would make up all kinds of bizarre stories and tons of random thoughts would pop into his head that he absolutely believed to be true, but weren't. He laughed loudly at things that didn't seem to be the least bit funny to me and I found it all very unnerving.

Eric would talk to solicitors, whether it was on the phone or at the front door. I knew that he would agree to buy whatever they were trying to sell him if I hadn't been there to tell him to just hang up. He seemed to have all the time and patience to talk on the phone about aluminum siding or a new phone plan. I wish he would have shown the same patience with our kids.

I always felt like I was waiting for things to show up in the mail that he ordered that I didn't know about. Thank goodness for the "Do Not Call list." I also had "no solicitor" signs plastered all over our front door.

Food, Marvelous Food

ERIC ALWAYS HAD a very healthy appetite and had always battled his weight. If you looked at pictures of him over the span of many years, you could see his weight fluctuate. When I first met him, Eric told me that, every year, he went on a diet for the whole month of February. When I asked him, "Why February?" He said, "Because it's the shortest month."

After his surgery, Eric's eating became a very bad problem. He would eat fast and furiously, wolfing down his food. To coin a phrase a friend of mine used to say, "Eric would eat like he was going to the chair." By the time I got my potato buttered and my meat cut, Eric's plate was so clean, it looked like you could put it right back into the cabinet.

It seemed he was unable to experience feeling full anymore because he would finish his own food and then reach over and start eating food off of the kids' plates. This drove the kids and me crazy. The kids started eating their food with one arm wrapped around their plate, protecting their food because they knew that their dad would reach over and eat it. *I always worried that they would develop some sort of eating disorder because of it.*

After his brain surgery, not only did he eat fast and steal food off the other plates, but because of his lack of short-term memory, he would forget that he had just eaten a meal and would look to find another one. He'd say, "When are we going to eat?" and I'd tell him, "You just ate." He would insist that he hadn't.

This was when I became the food police. Mealtime became very stressful. I had to change my serving habits and could never serve anything family style because Eric would eat, and eat, and eat until it was all gone. I also couldn't leave any pots on the stove top that might have had stew or something in them because when he would see a pot on the stove, once he finished the food on his plate, he would get up and serve himself another serving, again and again, until everything in the pot was gone.

I started putting everything inside the oven, whether it was cooked in the oven or not. There were several times I would find food in the oven the next day that I had forgotten about. I also learned, early on, that I couldn't clear any dishes when he was done eating. If I did, he would think that he didn't eat yet and would get up, get out a new plate, and serve himself some food. Even when I left the plate in front of him, he'd argue when I told him he had already eaten, saying, "No I did not." I really don't think he had the ability to feel full.

Anytime we went to a party where the hostess had a food table, it was a nightmare for me. He got very cranky when it came to the subject of food or when I tried to tell him he had enough and it was time to quit eating.

In October of 2005, a friend of ours had a Halloween party. Eric stood by the food table and shoveled the food in, nonstop. I tried to have him move and casually said, "Hey, Eric, why don't you move over to this side so other people can get in and have some snacks."

He sneered and very sarcastically said, "I can eat with my left hand, too, you know."

One year, they had a holiday party at Eric's rehab. I am sure no one monitored the volume of food Eric ate. We had plans to go out to dinner at an Italian restaurant with a group of our friends later that night. At dinner, Eric ate, and ate, and ate. I said a few times, "That's enough, let's get a doggie bag," but I was always worried that he'd yell and cause a scene about not wanting to quit eating.

When we got home that night, not long after he sat down in his chair, Eric projectile vomited across the family room and nearly hit the TV. He did, however, hit our wicker basket that held the newspapers and magazines. *Oh great! I'm married to Linda Blair.*

Eric was very slow to react. After the shock of what I had just witnessed wore off, I scrambled to clean both him and the room. *Have you ever tried to clean barf off a wicker basket? Let's just say we no longer have that basket.*

Another time, we were at our end-of-the-year softball banquet at a restaurant. There was one, long, rectangular table for our team. I sat on one side of Eric and our friend, Jim, sat on the other. As usual,

Eric wolfed down his meal and was done when everyone else was only half-way through theirs.

Toward the end of the meal, everyone started getting up to socialize and talk with other people at the table. When Jim got up, Eric ate what was left on Jim's plate. If Jim noticed, he was nice enough not to say anything. I was mortified.

Our New Normal

WE HAD GOTTEN INTO as much of a routine as you could with daily unpredictable behavior. Every night after I put the kids to bed, I would sit in my chair in the family room, Eric would be in his chair across from mine, either staring at the TV or sleeping and I'd think to myself, *Ahhh… I made it through another day.* I also thought, *Am I going to be sitting here one or two years from now just 'getting through the day'?*

I didn't want to live that way. I knew that for sure. This terrible thing, Eric's brain tumor, had damaged our lives as we knew it. Eric was altered and most likely would never be the same as he was pre-surgery. I knew I needed to concentrate on doing things he <u>could</u> do and things <u>we</u> could enjoy as a family. I needed to make the most of our lives now, after surgery. I needed to figure out our "new normal."

Our lives consisted of all the regular day-to-day activities, like those of most people. Our daily routine would start by Eric reading the newspaper. I use the term "read" loosely. He would read a few paragraphs, forget what he had read, and read the same thing over again.

I took Eric with me to run errands and tried to involve him with the kids as much as possible. He tried to help the kids with their homework, although his attention span was limited. We worked together in the yard. Eric was still confused and demonstrated bizarre behavior, but as time went on, it just became part of our lives, something we dealt with everyday.

Eric would sit with me at the kids' sports practices and games, while the repetitive questions came quickly and furiously. "What day was it?" "Why was I home from work today?" It just became part of our daily lives. We went on a lot of family bike rides and family walks. In the summer, we spent a lot of time at the public pool and had family game nights. These were the things we could do as a family.

One of our nephews got married in West Virginia and our daughter, Alex, was the flower girl. This was a big undertaking for me because we flew into Washington D.C. and rented a car to get to

West Virginia. These were things that pre-surgery, Eric would have taken care of, but now I had to do. I was nervous because I didn't know how Eric would handle the change in routine and surroundings. Throughout the wedding weekend, we were up early in the morning and stayed up late at night. There was a lot of action and activities and Eric did very well.

At the wedding reception, the disc jockey called all the married couples out on the dance floor. The disc jockey announced that all couples married less than four hours had to leave the dance floor, so of course the bride and groom had to leave the floor. Then he announced that all couples married less than two years had to exit the dance floor. Obviously, you can see where this was going. They were going to keep eliminating couples until the couple married the longest was left. The d.j. announced couples married less than five years had to get off the dance floor and Eric started pulling me off the floor. I told Eric that it wasn't our turn yet, that we were married eleven years and Eric said, "No way."

Next, it was couples married less than ten years and again Eric tried to lead me off of the dance floor. I told him again that we were married eleven years and he argued with me, saying, "I don't mind dancing with you if you want to dance, but I know we haven't been married eleven years."

Then he asked, "Do you really want to win this contest so much you would lie about how long we've been married?" *For the love of God. Yes, that's right Eric, this contest is super important to me.*

I remember thinking to myself, "Am I really trying to convince my husband how long we've been married?" Sometimes the reality of Eric's state of mind was like a slap in the face.

For Tommy's birthday, we met my brothers and my friend, Maureen, at a pizza place to celebrate. At the end of the evening, everyone left, except for Maureen and us. The kids were playing in the videogame area and we were sitting at the table talking. Eric picked up a plastic pitcher of diet soda and drank right out of the pitcher. I yelled, "Eric, what are you doing? You don't drink out of the pitcher. Use a cup."

Eric said, "I didn't know which cup was mine." This was the kind of behavior that happened just out of the blue. We never knew what Eric was thinking or what he would do.

The adoption agency through which we adopted both our kids had an annual summer picnic. Several years before Eric got sick, we hosted the picnic at our house. We went to the picnic after Eric's surgery and a friend named Kathy, whom we had met through the agency, came up to talk to me. She said that all those years ago, the minute she first met Eric and me, she felt that we were people she could hang out with. "Eric was so friendly and made me feel comfortable immediately. He talked to everyone and was very outgoing." She shared how sad she felt that this terrible thing had happened to Eric.

After she said that, I looked over and there was Eric, sitting in his lawn chair in the middle of the picnic, sleeping. She was right. It was very sad and I always admired her for saying to me what everyone was thinking. Including me.

For my 40th birthday, Maureen had us over to her house to celebrate. She made a great dinner and it was such a nice evening. It was so thoughtful of her to do that for me.

At the same time, I couldn't help thinking that my own husband hadn't really acknowledged my birthday. I knew he probably wasn't capable of it, but all I knew was I didn't like my bizarre, strange "new" husband. Adjusting to all of the side effects of Eric's brain tumor was difficult, to say the least.

One time, we went to a Mexican restaurant with three other couples for Maureen's birthday. We started at the bar, drinking margaritas, and then sat down for dinner. I was always on edge in this type of situation because these couples were not people we were really close with and I never knew what Eric might say or how he'd behave. They knew about Eric's history, but I was still nervous.

The night was going very well and Eric was doing fantastically. He was listening to people's stories, laughing at all the appropriate times and even threw in a few witty lines here and there. I couldn't believe it. Maureen and I exchanged surprised looks several times during the night as if to say, "Wow, Eric's doing great." I felt like I did in the old days when Eric and I went out to dinner with friends and enjoyed the night.

After dinner, the other couples had to leave, but Maureen, her husband Brian, Eric, and I stayed and had one more drink at the bar. Maureen and I whispered to each other how awesome it was to see Eric having such a good night. At the end of the night, we said goodbye to Maureen and Brian and left the restaurant. As we were walking through the parking lot, Eric had his arm around me and said, "Did you enjoy the movie?"

What? I couldn't believe my ears. Here I was basking in the glow of an awesome night and Eric asked me if I liked the movie. I stopped walking, turned around in the parking lot, and pointed to the giant restaurant marquis. I told him we weren't at a movie. I said we just had dinner to celebrate Maureen's birthday. Eric was looking at the sign and all he said was, "Oh." The whole ride home Eric slept and I cried.

The severity of Eric's injury always amazed me. In June of 2006, Ben Roethlisberger, quarterback for the Pittsburgh Steelers, crashed while riding his motorcycle without wearing a helmet. He had a broken jaw, a broken nose, and was in surgery for seven hours. I remember hearing this story on the news. They reported that after the accident, Ben was awake, alert, and oriented.

I marveled at the fact that Eric's surgery was a scheduled surgery, performed under a controlled setting. There was no horrible crash or accident causing a hard impact, yet I didn't know if Eric would ever be alert and oriented again.

PART THREE

You're Killing Me with the Memory Thing

For the Love of the Game?

The Episodes – Eight Hours – February, 2004

IN FEBRUARY OF 2004, the first of what I had come to refer to as "Episodes" occurred. These episodes could be described as a temporary derailment of Eric's common sense—an immediate, intense obsession focused on one particular subject. It was as if his mind was hit hard with a barrage of thoughts that he couldn't repress. Eric was very intense during these episodes and most of the time was unable to be distracted.

The first episode started at 5:00 p.m. Eric said he had to go play softball and started looking for his mitt. There were two problems with this thought. First of all, it was February in Chicago, not quite the height of softball season and second, it had been 18 years since Eric had played softball.

He searched the front hall closets, then went out to the garage and checked the minivan. First, he checked the front passenger-side floor, then opened the sliding door and checked under all the seats. While he was opening the back hatch of the van, I went to the basement, found his mitt, cleaned off the cobwebs and gave it to him, thankful to end the craziness.

Without breaking stride, Eric muttered something about needing his cleats and headed for the basement. I knew I was in trouble because his cleats didn't exist. How would I be able to convince him? For the next hour, he walked laps around our first floor. He walked through our living room and checked under the cushions of the chairs and couch. *Isn't that where everyone keeps their baseball cleats?*

Then he walked into our family room where our kids were watching TV and told our daughter to get off the chair she was sitting on. He looked under the chair cushion. He went back to the garage and checked all areas of the van. Then he repeated "the lap"—living room, family room, garage, checking all the seat cushions and same spots over and over, as if the cleats would all of a sudden appear under the couch cushion this time.

I attempted to distract Eric while he was doing his laps, so he would stop. I asked him to sit down for a minute, but he refused. I offered him something to eat, which he also refused. Eric never refused food! I realized it was going to be a rough night.

Eric's parents were in town and witnessed the whole debacle. They tried to distract Eric, too, but with no success. We tried reasoning with Eric. We tried yelling at him, the tough love approach. We yelled at him and told him to snap out of it. Nothing worked.

Since he had taken to dressing in layers, he was wearing a short-sleeved t-shirt under a long sleeved t-shirt under a sweatshirt. While he was doing his laps, he also had on his black, winter, leather jacket.

About an hour later, as he walked past me, I asked, "What are you doing, Eric?"

His response surprised me. "I have to take that box of stuff to that guy." *How's that for vague statement of the year?*

Apparently, the obsessive thought changed from his softball cleats to taking a box of stuff to some guy. What "stuff" and what "guy," we had no idea. The laps continued, searching for "the box." He would not sit down and became progressively more frantic. Eric felt that it was getting late and the guy needed this box that he couldn't find.

About 9:00 p.m., I called our friend Rick to come over. My thought was that if someone new was in the house, it might distract Eric long enough to forget this obsession of searching for "the box."

Rick arrived quickly and I said, "Look who is here Eric; Rick has come to visit us. Why don't you get him a beer, and one for yourself while you're at it?"

Eric said, "I can't. I have to find the box. It's getting late." The laps continued.

I got Rick a beer and he watched with Eric's parents and me, in amazement, as Eric mumbled to himself, frantically dashing from room to room.

I went to the garage and told Eric how rude he was being. I told him his friend had come to visit him and the least he could do was go inside, take his coat off, sit down, and have a beer with his friend. He walked into the kitchen and got himself a beer, but never sat down.

He asked Rick, "Do you know where that box is I had earlier? I need to bring it to this guy's house and I can't find it anywhere." Rick told him no, that he hadn't seen any box and then Eric put his beer down and continued his laps.

When I pressed Eric and asked him who the guy was and what was in the box he needed to give to him, he couldn't come up with any details.

The constant, obsessive searching continued. I tried something new. I said to Eric a few minutes later, "Hey Eric, the guy called and said not to bring the box of stuff over tonight because it's late and his wife is sleeping and he doesn't want to wake her up, so he'll just get the box from you tomorrow."

Eric stopped and thought for a minute. He said, "I didn't hear the phone ring."

I told him it rang when he was in the garage. *I figured if he can make up some guy then I can play the game too!*

I was giving myself accolades and thinking how clever I was, when Eric responded, "Well, he just called back and said he does want me to bring it tonight after all."

My heart sank. I thought I finally was going to put a stop to this madness. It was now 11:00 p.m. I thanked Rick for coming over and sent him home. I sent Grandma and Grandpa up to bed and turned all the lights off on the first floor, except one in the family room. I told Eric that I'd be lying on the couch until he was ready to go up to bed.

The laps around the first floor and trips to the garage continued. Finally, at 1:00 a.m., I told Eric I was going up to bed. I went upstairs to our bedroom and listened at the door. I heard him still doing laps and opening and closing the door to the garage.

About 15 minutes later, Eric came up to our bedroom looking for the box of stuff for the guy. This nightmare was now eight hours old and I couldn't take much more. I took Eric by the shoulders and put my face right up against his. We were nose to nose. I asked, "Eric, do you love me?"

He seemed like a caged animal trying to move. He told me he loved me, but he had to get the box of stuff to the guy and he needed to find it so he could go.

I told Eric I felt like he didn't love me anymore and asked him if he could please lie down with me for just 10 minutes. I knew that after eight hours of constant pacing and sweating, he had to be exhausted and once he lay down, he would pass out.

Eric begrudgingly agreed to lie down with me and within two minutes, he started snoring. I felt bad he was lying in bed in his jeans and leather jacket but I didn't dare wake him to have him change.

I went downstairs and every light on the first floor was on, the garage door was open and so were all the doors of the van. I closed everything up, turned off all the lights, and lay down next to him.

My mind was racing, even though I was emotionally and physically exhausted. I couldn't believe tonight's ordeal lasted eight and a half hours. What was happening to Eric's mind? Is this a one-time thing or will I have the pleasure of more episodes in the future? Fifteen minutes after Eric fell asleep, he woke up and looked down at himself. I thought, "Oh God, please, no. I can't do this anymore."

I asked Eric what was wrong and he said with a confused look on his face, "I fell asleep with my clothes on." He swung his legs over the side of the bed and got up and I got a sick feeling in my stomach. I thought, here we go again. I asked him where he was going and he said, "To brush my teeth and put my pajamas on." He did exactly that, returned back to bed and fell fast asleep. There was never another word about tonight's eight-and-a-half hours of frantic behavior. Like many things since his surgery, it was wiped from Eric's memory.

The Little "Magic" Pill

(in addition to all the others)

THE NEXT DAY, I CALLED the neurosurgeon's office and explained what happened the night before. I told them I needed something I could give him if he ever had another one of these episodes. They called in an anti-anxiety pill prescription into our pharmacy. I couldn't believe how small the pills were. They were one milligram and they told me it would take about 25 - 30 minutes to take effect. They said it would relax Eric and take the edge off.

The first time I had to use one of the pills came only five days later. It was Sunday afternoon, February 22nd and unseasonably warm weather for Chicago. I was outside in the front yard with the kids and they were playing with their neighborhood friends.

Eric came storming out of the house. Obviously agitated, he yelled to me, "Where is the basketball?"

I asked him why he was looking for it and he told me he had a basketball game to get to.

Eric had always hated to play basketball. I couldn't get him to play the game if I had put a gun to his head. Yet here he was, frantically looking for the basketball because he had a game.

Eric had the key to our van. He got in and started the engine. Although I told the other mom to keep the kids on her driveway, I told Eric that there were kids behind the van and that he couldn't pull out. He told me, very angrily, "Get them the hell out of the way or I'll run them down."

The rage and mean personality that Eric demonstrated was so completely opposite of the pre-surgery, gentle, kind, loving Eric I married. He would really have to be pushed far to even raise his voice, let alone behave in such an outrageous manner. It was also a change from the distant behavior he demonstrated since he arrived home from the hospital.

I thought, "Who is this horrible person who has taken over my husband's body? <u>My</u> Eric would never say anything like this."

I got in the passenger seat and eventually reached over and grabbed the keys out of the ignition. I ran through the house while taking the van key off Eric's key ring and stashed it in a kitchen drawer.

At this point, he was enraged. You could say, "Madder than a wet hen." The kids were with the neighbors outside so they didn't hear his ranting about how I better give him the keys or else.

When I finally gave him his keys back and he saw that the van key was missing, he went nuts. At this point, he very much resembled Jack Nicholson in "The Shining." He yelled and screamed and paced back and forth and asked me why I was doing this to him.

Eric's mother, who was still in town, told me, "Give him a pill, give him a pill."

In the midst of his fury, I told him he hadn't taken his medicine yet. He grabbed the glass of water and pill that I handed to him, swallowing the pill without any question as to what it was or why he was taking a pill in the middle of the day when he usually didn't.

It took almost one full hour for the pill to take effect. He seemed to just relax and mellow out. Eventually, he quit talking about having to get in the car, and he sat in his chair, watched sports, and fell asleep.

All I could think about was thank God for this little miracle pill. I couldn't handle another eight-hour episode. I also found it a little funny that in the middle of a tantrum, Eric took the pill without question. Thank goodness! Because in that state of mind, I certainly couldn't force him to take it if he didn't want to.

Just two days later, at 7:00 p.m. Eric told his mom and me that he had to go to a softball meeting, *(remember, he hadn't played softball in 18 years)* to "bring the roster to the guys." I told Eric he didn't have a softball meeting and he got angry instantly. His mom and I recognized it as the beginning of another episode, so I gave him a pill, which he took without any hesitation.

I asked Eric to go upstairs to read books to our kids before they went to bed (a stall tactic to give the pill time to work). With a huff and angry mumblings about how I didn't care if he missed the meeting, up he went, to spend some time with the children.

When he came back downstairs, there was no more talk of going anywhere and he sat down and joined us watching TV. We watched Frasier and he promptly fell asleep in his chair.

Softball Anyone?

ALTHOUGH ERIC RANTED about having a basketball game that one time, softball was his sport of choice. It was strange how this obsession with softball entered our lives and became one of the toughest issues I dealt with during Eric's illness.

When Eric was in his early 20s, living in Pittsburgh, he played in a softball league with his buddies, and loved it. He used to tell me stories of how much fun they had in those days. I often wondered if he was thinking of those days while he was having his brain surgery because softball was carved in his mind and nothing could wipe it out of his head.

It was like torture. It started around the same time everyday. As it got closer to 3:30 in the afternoon, I always felt my stomach tighten and the feeling of dread mount. I knew what was coming. If I could predict the lottery numbers the way I could predict Eric's behavior those days, I'd be a rich woman.

Eric would stretch out his arm, look at his watch, and as if reading from a script, he would say, "I have no idea where the game is tonight." I heard that simple sentence **almost everyday for three and a half years.**

Eric would then get our address book out of the drawer and start calling his friends, asking if they knew where the game was, no matter where they lived. His friends would tell Eric they didn't play softball and Eric would say, "Well, you must not be on the team."

We were in Chicago and he'd call Pittsburgh and Virginia to see if they were going to play in the game that night. I would say to Eric, "It's 4 p.m. on a Tuesday night in Chicago. Do you really think someone from Pittsburgh or Virginia would fly here on a weeknight for a softball game?" He then told me that they did it all the time. *Ug.*

There was no reasoning with him on this subject. Actually, there was no reasoning with him on any subject. He was incapable of reasoning. He always got his different groups of friends mixed up. He'd call his golf buddies and ask them if they were playing softball that night. They would tell him they never played softball together, but he didn't believe them.

Because of Eric's lack of short-term memory, he would call a friend about softball, hang up, call someone else, and then call the first guy again. His friends would get six calls from Eric within a ten-minute time period. All his friends were incredibly gracious and patient.

I would try distracting Eric to get him to forget about softball, but most of the time it didn't work. When he started up on softball, I would call his parents in South Carolina and have them talk to him for a while, in hopes that he'd forget about softball. It rarely worked. The softball obsession occurred year round. There could be three feet of snow piled up outside and he'd be calling people about softball. When I'd point out that softball was only played in spring and summer, Eric would tell me they shoveled off the fields in the winter. *Ahhh*. I would get our mitts and play catch with Eric outside to see if that would satisfy his obsession, but it never did.

Neighbors to the Rescue — A Valiant Attempt!

OUR FRIENDS IN THE NEIGHBORHOOD came up with the idea to put together a co-ed softball team to play in our Park District league in hopes to fulfill Eric's softball needs. It didn't work. I would catch Eric checking his watch during or co-ed games and then he'd ask me how much longer I thought the game would last because he had to get to his men's game. *For the love of God.*

The ironic part of the whole situation was that when we did play our co-ed games, Eric stunk. He was terrible. To his credit, half the problem was that his vision was so bad, he could hardly see. He was a big hitter when he made contact, but then he was slower than molasses running the bases. I just figured if you fantasized and obsessed about playing softball you would at least be good at it. Nope.

We named our co-ed team "The Apollos" because Eric said that was the name of his men's league team. We had no idea where he came up with that name because his buddies with whom he played twenty-some years earlier told me their team name was "Coppers" after a company in Pittsburgh that sponsored them.

Although our hopes of fulfilling Eric's softball obsession with our co-ed team did not work, we all had a good time playing and I will be forever grateful to The Apollos for being so nice to Eric.

Refinancing

IF YOU WERE JUST LOOKING AT ERIC, he appeared perfectly fine. Even his vocabulary was very good and he presented as very "normal." It was only after talking to him for about fifteen to twenty minutes that you realized something was not quite right. Even then, you couldn't put your finger on what exactly it was.

Not too long after Eric came home from the hospital, we refinanced our mortgage. After the mortgage was approved, we had a meeting with our banker to sign all the paperwork. I was a nervous wreck going into this meeting, wondering what Eric would say, how he would act, and what he would do. I always seemed to be on edge, not knowing how situations would play out. As the meeting went on, I was pleasantly surprised at how subdued Eric was. There was small talk about the weather as we signed our names on every form, over and over, passing it from banker, to me, to Eric, and putting them in a pile. I was thinking to myself, *Wow! It has been about forty minutes and Eric has been great. This guy has no idea what Eric has been through. He has no idea that Eric had brain surgery and was completely different from how he used to be.* I was amazed at how well this meeting went.

The banker left the table to make copies of all the documents for us to take home. Who knew? I worried for nothing. The banker returned with a folder that contained all of our documents, shook our hands, and thanked us for our business. I was grinning from ear to ear. The banker probably thought I was overly thrilled to refinance. Little did he know that it was sheer relief on my part.

As we started to turn and leave, Eric turned back around and said to the man, "Are we driving you home?" The confused look on the banker's face was priceless.

I hooked my arm in Eric's elbow, pulled and said, "No Eric, he's driving himself home."

I whisked Eric out of the bank, into the parking lot, into the van, and got on the street as fast as I possibly could.

While driving home I started to giggle about the look on the banker's face. He's probably still scratching his head wondering why his client thought he'd be driving him home.

Medical Mumbo Jumbo... or How One Word Can Bring Inner Peace

I'M SURE YOU ALREADY KNOW that this book is not here to teach you a bunch of medical terms or educate you on the inner-workings of the brain. However, a few terms can really be helpful for providing some insight to our story. We humans like naming things. It helps us communicate and order our world. For me, one simple word helped me regain just a tiny bit of sanity amidst this chaotic life I had fallen into…

While Eric was in the outpatient rehab facility, I had a meeting with the counselors and they provided me with a large binder that contained many articles about brain injury. The binder remained at the facility, but they offered to make copies of any articles that caught my interest.

One particular article brought me to tears because, until I discovered it, I felt no one knew what I was going through. This article was an exact outline of our situation. It discussed the severe memory deficit and something called "confabulation." The next several short paragraphs are taken from an article entitled "Severe Cognitive Communication Impairments," written by Alice Johansen, M. S., CCC-SLP.

> **Memory.** To communicate successfully we need to remember what was said previously. We have to remember to whom we are talking, and about what. We contribute to the conversation by recalling past experiences. We also will hold information in our heads to tell someone later.
>
> When their memory functions are severely impaired, individuals with TBI (traumatic brain injury) do not remember what they or you have said already. They will ask the same question over and over. They

have trouble remembering what has happened from moment to moment. Imagine how frustrating this can be to a caregiver on a day-to-day basis!

You said it Alice Johansen.

Imagine how frightening this might be to the person with the memory impairment! Our sense of ourselves depends on remembering where we came from, what just happened, where we are now and whom we are with. This ability keeps us oriented and grounded in reality.

When information gaps appear, the individual with TBI may fill them in with something. The information "fillers" however, often are untrue. In some cases the person may deny having a family or being in the hospital. Family members are often bewildered and frightened by such stories. The speech pathologist or neuro-psychologist may refer to this kind of occurrence as "confabulation." The individual may get angry or agitated when corrected on errors of fact.

Did you catch that? Did you catch what Alice Johansen, my new best friend, wrote? She said that "when information gaps appear, the individual fills them up with 'fillers' that are often untrue."

Often untrue! Untrue, like: horse selling, nose jobs, carpooling with bankers, going to work at a non-existent job, fantasy social life, and an obsessive softball addiction. *God bless you Alice Johansen!*

"Confabulation"—an actual term! Up until I read that article, I was using terms like: wacky, nut job, crazy, loony. But now I know there is an actual term for all this stuff that Eric was doing. *Confabulation.* I know it won't fix it, but at least I had a name for it now. A name. Hallelujah! *Sometimes it's the small things in life that make your day.*

Finding Anixter / "Training" Eric

IN AUGUST, THE OUTPATIENT REHAB personnel informed me that they had to discharge Eric from the program. They said that due to his short-term memory deficit, they had to repeat too much and felt they weren't making any progress. They thought it was a waste of the therapists' time.

I didn't know what I was going to do. I had to find somewhere for Eric to go. He certainly couldn't spend the rest of his life at home all day. He was only 43 years old. He needed his brain stimulated and he needed to feel like he had a purpose. This started my dialing for dollars campaign.

I called every agency and association I could find. After explaining Eric's age and situation, the typical line I would get was, "We don't deal with anything like that, but I'll give you a phone number you can call to somewhere that might."

I can't tell you how many places and programs I called. I finally found out about Anixter Center and their program called "New Focus," which specifically served people with brain injuries.

Eric, his mom and I met with the head of Anixter's "New Focus" program. After our interview, we were told Eric was accepted. We were so lucky! It was a government-funded program with a maximum attendance of one year. They performed frequent evaluations and held progress meetings with the client and their families to determine how long the client would participate in the program.

We were ecstatic. Finally, there was a place for Eric to go that was structured specifically for people with brain injuries. They certainly wouldn't fault him for not being able to remember. I'm sure he wouldn't be the only one.

There was only one problem. The program was located downtown and there was no transportation provided. Spending a minimum of 2 ½ hours in the car each day with two kids was not practical. So that left us with one option: Teach Eric how to take the train downtown and then walk the eight blocks from the train to the program building. Would that ever work?

Eric's cousin, Mary, was out of work at the time and living downtown. She played a major role in training Eric.

Each day, Mary, Eric's mom and I took turns getting on the train with Eric, reminding him at which stop to get off. The train ride lasted about 40 minutes one-way.

After we arrived at his stop, we walked with Eric and discussed all of the landmarks along the way. "Eric, now we're passing the Star Car Wash and going over the bridge. Now we're passing all the blue painted doors of Finkle Steel on our left. See the sculpture of a big screw...here's where we turn left. (*Thank goodness for the sculpture because there was no street sign.*) Now we'll go up to the next side street, take a quick right and then we'll go up into the door with the blue awning. Here's where we tell Tommy the security guard to call up to Sarah Nicolson and let her know to come down and get you." This was the dialogue everyday as we walked with Eric to rehab.

Mary picked Eric up in the afternoon, collected him from one of the therapists in the lobby, and reversed the morning dialogue back to the train platform. "A quick right turn out the door to the end of the street, turn left, to the big screw, turn right, past all the blue doors of Finkel Steel over the bridge past the car wash under the viaduct to the train platform."

This was the routine for about one month. Then we started the weaning process. First we rode with Eric, but had him lead the way. Then, we ghost rode on the train, watching Eric from another car, making sure he got off the train at the right stop. We followed behind him at a safe distance seeing that he made it to the rehab building. We hoped Finkel Steel never repainted their doors a different color because Eric really relied on those blue doors as landmarks.

Thank goodness for technology. I gave Eric a cell phone and once I put him on the train by himself, I waited a little while and called him when his stop was about five minutes away. I would hear the announcement for his stop in the background and I'd tell him he had to get off the train and then I would stay on the phone with him while he walked to the rehab building. That cell phone was my lifeline to Eric...when it worked.

The Blind Leading the...

IN MARCH OF 2004, I brought along Tommy when I took Eric to the train station in Palatine (Grandma and Grandpa were still visiting and were home with Alex). We were waiting for the train and I noticed a blind man pass us, walking with his guide dog. I thought he just got off a train, but then I noticed he passed us and stood about three feet to our left and faced the train tracks. He was obviously waiting for the train. I thought, "What the heck..." and asked, "Sir, do you mind if I ask you if you are waiting for the 7:24 train that is going downtown?"

He replied, "Yes."

I asked, "Do you take the train everyday?" He said he took it 3 – 4 times per week.

I explained, "I'm not trying to give you the 3rd degree, but the reason I'm asking is my husband Eric is standing here and he is recovering from a brain injury. He has no short-term memory as a result of his injury. He is starting a new rehab program downtown and has to get off the train at the Clybourne stop, but he doesn't always remember to get off the train. He mistakenly traveled all the way downtown last week. Do you think you could remind Eric to get off at Clybourne?"

I explained that I had a cell phone and would call Eric myself, but told him I was trying to put as many backup plans into place so that he got off the train where he was supposed to.

Bill-the-Blind-Man (which is how we lovingly referred to him) said it would be no problem and agreed that it was a good idea to have several plans in place.

After our initial conversation, we stood at the train stop and talked while waiting for the train. I introduced our son, Tommy, and myself to Bill, and Bill introduced his guide dog, Abner.

The train arrived and I told Eric to sit by Bill because he would be helping him remember when to get off the train. I said goodbye to Eric and told him to have a good day.

Bill started to board the train and when he reached the third step he looked over his shoulder and said "Eric, you there?" and Eric said, "Yes."

Bill said, "Come on, we're going to sit over here." Eric followed him.

As usual, I called Eric on his cell phone and talked with him until he got to his stop. When the Clybourne stop was announced, I heard Bill-the-Blind-Man in the background say, "Eric, this is your stop."

Bill did what I asked. It was so nice of him. Tears came to my eyes just thinking how nice it was of this total stranger to help Eric out.

While driving home from the train station, I laughed out loud to myself. "OK. I just asked a blind man to help my fully sighted husband get off the train at the right stop." I couldn't stop laughing. I thought how funny the people on the train must have thought it was when Bill said, "Hey Eric, this is your stop." I'm sure it got some double takes. I also thought that after I asked Bill to help Eric, Bill might have been thinking, "Hey lady, can't you tell I've got enough of my own problems? Do I look like I have time to take care of your husband too?! I'm sure he wasn't thinking that. He was too nice.

The next day, Bill-the-Blind-Man wasn't at the train station. Of course, it figured. I was so happy that I had this new back up plan in place with Bill and the very next day he wasn't there. Oh well. I put Eric on the train, called him on his cell phone and he made it fine.

I arranged for the rehab staff to call me each day when Eric arrived, so I didn't worry that he never made it. Not only did I worry about Eric getting off at the right train stop and making the eight-block walk, but the building the program was in was a huge, city-block-long building. I got lost in it trying to find the program, so I pictured Eric wandering around the building, lost for hours.

I also talked to Eric via cell phone on the way home. They released him from the program at 2:15 p.m. and I always called him at 2:20 p.m. for the last part of the walk to the train platform, until he stepped on the train.

One day, I called Eric at 2:25 p.m. and asked him where he was on his walk home. Eric said, "I'm in the parking lot of Anixter." I was panicked because he should have been almost to the platform by then and I didn't want him to miss his train.

I said, "Just in the parking lot, what are you doing there?"

Eric said, "Well, I'm in this guy's car."

I almost had a heart attack. I screamed, "What? You're in someone's car? Who?" I ordered Eric to hand him the cell phone. I laugh now, looking back on it, because had this person been up to no good, he would not have let Eric talk to me on the phone.

The man whose car Eric was in, told me his name was Rafael and said he was in Eric's class. He told me he saw Eric leave rehab, but that when he left himself, Eric was just hanging around the parking lot, so he offered Eric a ride.

I don't know why Eric was just hanging around the parking lot. Maybe he thought Mary was going to pick him up?

I directed Rafael to the train platform. Eric got out of the car and said, "Thanks."

Then I heard Rafael say, "Eric, I can take you everyday because I have to come this way."

I thought to myself, "I'll deal with that later."

Since Eric was driven to the train platform by car, he wasn't facing the right direction and wasn't sure where to go to get up the stairs to the correct platform. I directed him to go to the stoplight, then turn around and find the stairs like he usually did. He told me, "No, these stairs say Harvard-Chicago. These are it."

I yelled, "No Eric, they are not the right stairs. You need the stairs that say Northwest Suburbs." He started to walk to the light and passed the right set of stairs that said Northwest Suburbs. He finally walked up them with only about two minutes to spare.

Scary, scary, scary because when I asked Eric whose car he was in, he couldn't tell me. Does that mean he would get in a car with anyone? Did he know the guy was from his class and he just couldn't remember his name? I didn't know.

After that day, his walks were fine. I still talked to him on the phone, which was kind of a crutch, but if that is what I had to do to avoid him wandering around Chicago, then it was okay by me. I sat at home and imagined an "Amber Alert" out for Eric Posey. A 6'2", 250 lb. man is missing… Be on alert. If you see this grown man, call his wife because she's losing her mind!

From the first day we met Bill-the-Blind-Man, Eric constantly called him Mike. He thought that Bill was our friend, Mike Weber. Eric argued with me and insisted that Bill was Mike. I told Bill, one morning at the train stop, that he resembled a friend of ours named, Mike Weber, and before I could finish the story, Bill said, "So that's why he keeps calling me Mike."

I cannot begin to tell you how kind it was for Bill to help Eric out on the train. Bill had been taking the train downtown for many years and had many friends. On days when he wasn't on the train, a group of ladies, who were friends with Bill, would watch out for Eric and remind him about his stop. They were all such kind, nice people.

The last week of July, I put Eric on the train. Bill-the-Blind-Man was not on the train. I called Eric at 8:00 a.m., as I usually did, and the name of the train stop I heard announced in the background didn't make sense. The first thing Eric asked me when I called him was "Where are you?"

I told him I was at home and he said, "I'm trying to get there."

I knew immediately something was wrong. I listened and realized Eric got off the train and got on another train coming back toward home. I asked him if he did that and he said, "Well, this morning is a little foggy."

While on the cell phone with him, I guided him to get off at the next stop, and ask at the station what track he needed in order to head back toward downtown. This particular day, Eric ended up at Anixter only about one hour late. The positive thing was that Eric knew how to get off the train and catch one going in the direction he wanted.

Those Pesky Commuting Errors... or Divine Intervention — Friday, March 26th, 2004

I DIDN'T LIKE TO SEND ERIC downtown with a lot of money in his money clip. He didn't really need much money because I packed his lunch and he had a monthly train pass. Plus, in my opinion, he was traveling through some rough areas.

I knew Eric was very confused in the morning. Two weird things happened on this day. Eric asked me if I had any money I could give him. He had nine dollars on him. I only had a twenty-dollar bill and Eric insisted on having it. I gave it to him and figured the worst-case scenario was that he would lose twenty-nine dollars. I figured I had been through worse.

I took Eric to the train station by myself because Grandma and Grandpa were still in town. While we were sitting on the bench at the train station, Eric asked, "Where are we?" I asked him to think hard and take a guess as to where we were.

"Chicago?" he asked.

"Yes honey, Chicago," I replied. "We are at the Palatine train station and you are getting on the 7:24 train. You'll get off at the Clybourne exit and walk to Anixter. You're going to your rehab program."

I put him on the train, called him on his cell phone early in the ride, and told him I would call again in about ten minutes. When I did, the phone rang and rang and rang and then went into voicemail. I hung up and tried again; voicemail again.

At 8:45 a.m., the people from Anixter called and said he hadn't shown up yet. My heart jumped into my throat and I called his cell phone again. Finally, I got hold of Eric. It was pretty loud in the background. I asked Eric where he was. He paused, and responded, "Madison and Wabash."

I thought I was going to have a heart attack. I said, "What? Where are you going?"

Eric said, "I don't know."

I said to Eric, "You've got to turn around and get back to the train station. Do you know where it is?"

In an agitated tone he said, "I'll just turn around and go back where I came from." I didn't know if he really knew how to get back to the train and I certainly didn't know how to direct him.

I told Eric to hustle because he had to get back to the station and get on the 9:00 a.m. train that would take him back one train stop to the Clybourne exit, where he should have gotten off the first time. Soon, it became apparent to me that he was too far away and wouldn't make it back in time for the 9 a.m. and the next train was one hour later.

I said, "We have to change our plan of action. You will have to hail a cab."

He said "Ok," but then he stopped talking.

I said, "Eric, you need to hail a cab."

He said, "Two just went right by me."

I asked, "Do you have your hand up in the air?"

He yelled back, "Yes, I have my hand up in the air," in a very aggravated tone. Then he told me he had to cross the street and hail a cab from the other side. That scared me to death because I remember reading that it was very common for people with brain injuries to get hit by cars. Eric made it and shortly hailed a cab.

I gave Eric the address, which he repeated to the cab driver. I asked Eric to give the cab driver the cell phone so I could talk to the driver directly but Eric said, "I'm not going to do that."

I kept asking Eric, "What does the meter say now? What does the meter say now?" Thank goodness he asked for that extra money in the morning. *Strange huh?*

He got to Anixter and figured out how to enter the building from the main road, because he usually went in the side door when he walked from the train platform.

I had my home telephone in one ear talking to the therapist from Anixter, and my cell phone in the other talking to Eric. What chaos.

Later that morning, I heard on the news that the 9:00 a.m. train that Eric missed to go back another stop, crashed into another train coming out of the train yard and some people were injured and had to go to the hospital. Hmmm. First Eric asked for extra money that morning, which he ended up needing to pay for the cab, then the train that I wanted him to get on, but missed, crashed. *Divine intervention? Maybe.*

Gym Shoes or Florsheims? April 2004

I WAS ALWAYS LISTENING to make sure the water wasn't running for another shower each morning, and worrying that Eric was dressing for work or calling into a job that he hadn't had for several years. It was all very tedious.

In April of 2004, Eric would get up in the morning and get dressed in a suit and tie because he thought he had to go to work. Never mind that he hadn't worked in over a year. Also, in his mind, he was still working at the job he had for 18 years, rather than at the last job he had before his surgery.

He would come downstairs all dressed up and when I'd explain that he was going to a rehab program because of his brain tumor, he would get very angry and refuse to believe me.

He would say to me, "Wendy, why are you telling me that? You know darn well that I work at P&O."

He also started calling the office repeatedly asking to talk to his old secretary to pick up any messages she had for him. Yes, he remembered the office phone number! I thought this was incredible. His secretary no longer worked there either, but there were some employees who still remained from the days when Eric was there, including his colleague, Janet.

I felt so bad for Janet. People who didn't deal with Eric on a regular basis after his brain surgery, didn't know how to handle him. They didn't know if they should tell him the truth or go along with whatever he was saying. I spoke with Janet and others at the office, apologizing for Eric's calls and told them to tell him the truth about his current situation and that he no longer worked at the company.

Of course I always tried to stop him from calling, but there were many times when I'd hear Eric talking on the phone with the office. Talk about loyalty. He had gotten fired as part of a "restructuring" and here he was calling in for his messages. *Ug.*

When my mom was in town, we would sit at the kitchen table and listen to the water running for Eric's first shower of the morning.

The master bathroom was located directly above the kitchen and we could hear him walking around in the bathroom getting ready for the day. My mom and I would play a game we called "gym shoes or Florsheims." We'd each pick what type of shoe we thought Eric put on for the day based on the noise they made on the bathroom floor. Gym shoes would mean he dressed for rehab. "Florsheims" meant he dressed for work.

This game was just another way to find a few laughs in a very *un*funny situation. If we didn't laugh, we'd cry.

Change in Behavior: Agitated

I HAD STARTED TO NOTICE A CHANGE in Eric's behavior. When he first came home from the hospital, he had been very passive, borderline zombie-ish with a faraway, blank stare. There was no life behind his eyes. Early on, Eric had been very agreeable.

Now, a year later, my gentle giant of a husband was easily agitated, cranky and unpleasant to be around. Every response he had was delivered with an edgy, mean tone. He would sit in the family room and watch cartoons with the kids. It wasn't as if he was actually watching "with" the kids. There was no interaction with them on his part.

I would say to him "Eric, you're 44 years old and you're watching cartoons," and he would reply in a very snippy tone, "Yes, and I like them."

I remember once, on a warm day, Eric was outside with a heavy sweatshirt on and our neighbor said, "Eric, you've got to be hot with that shirt on."

Eric said very rudely and sarcastically, "Yes and I think I'm going to put on a heavy coat over it."

I remember thinking, "You can sweat your balls off for all I care." *You can tell where my level of patience was that day.*

Eric Goes For A Spin - April 6, 2004

ERIC WOULD COME HOME from Anixter and start right up with softball. It didn't help that he came home right around 3:30 p.m., which was the time he usually started his obsession. A doctor told me that the softball obsession sounded very much like "sun downing." This was a term I had never heard before. It was explained to me that "sun downing" was a term used with Alzheimer's patients to describe behavior difficulties that occur in the late afternoon or evening. It sure seemed to fit Eric's situation.

I used the anti-anxiety medication on Eric for softball, but he seemed to build up immunity to it. It made Eric tired, but the intensity of his obsession was stronger and usually won out.

It was a Tuesday in April. Eric went to Anixter, then we did yard work and took out the garbage when he got home. I kept ignoring Eric's obsessing about softball. First I said, "No you don't," and then I would give him something else to do to take his mind off it.

I had a pork tenderloin in the oven and after our work outside I said, "Ok Eric, we're going in to eat dinner."

He said, "I don't think I've got time to eat. I have softball." He said he thought it was in Lake Zurich, a neighboring town.

I ignored that comment and we went in. I had everybody clean up for dinner.

After dinner, we were clearing the dishes and I thought I had dodged the softball bullet, but no such luck. I told Eric that we needed to give the kids a bath and he said angrily, "Wendy I've got softball, I can't help you!"

I said, "No you don't Eric," and nonchalantly ignored him. I put the kids in the bathtub and Eric continued to insist that he had softball. I just kept saying, "No you don't, Eric."

Eric said, "I'm going." I told him he couldn't go, he didn't have softball and he had to help me with the kids. I took them out of the tub and told Eric he had to dry them off.

He said, "I've got to go," and headed downstairs. I went downstairs after him and followed him into the garage. Eric got in the van and started it.

I said to Eric, "Roll down the window." Then, I sternly said to him, "Look. You haven't driven in a year. If you kill someone you are going to be in huge trouble. If you take off, I'm going to have to call someone."

He said, "Who are you going to call?"

I said "I don't know, but do not go anywhere," and I went in the house and watched from the window. Sure enough, he pulled out of the driveway and drove off. It was 6:40 p.m. on a Tuesday night. I was terrified. I was thinking, "Oh my God."

I ran upstairs and finished drying off the kids. Our daughter, Alex, started firing all kinds of questions at me. "Where's Daddy?"

I told her, "He took a little ride looking for a softball game."

She said, "He can't drive. What's going to happen? I want my daddy," all in a panicked tone. "He can't drive. How are we going to find him?"

I said, "Alex, please don't worry." (*Of course I was a wreck.*)

I put their PJs on them and I thought to myself, *What do I do now?* I called my brother, Butch. He wasn't home, so I left him a message. I called Eric's parents. They weren't home, and I left them a message, too. (*Why the heck I called them I have no idea. There's not a lot they could have done from South Carolina.*)

I called our friend Rick and told him what was going on and asked him to be available as a back up should the police call or Eric needs to be picked up. He said, "No problem."

He asked me if I had called the police yet and I told him I didn't want to raise a red flag. I was worried I would be shinning a light on our situation here. Would they think I couldn't handle Eric and think to take him from the home? I wasn't thinking straight, but I was afraid to call the police.

Then I called Maureen. Both she and her husband thought I should call the police. I told them my concerns about calling the police and she called her sister-in-law, who also agreed that I should call the police and just let them know what's going on. At this point, I was really nervous because it was 7:20 p.m. and there was still no sign of Eric.

I put a videotape in for the kids to keep them busy. Then Alex yelled over and said "Mommy, Mommy, I felt warm in my pants and look…" I looked down at her and she had diarrhea running down her legs underneath her nightgown. She had gotten herself so worked up that she had diarrhea. Kids are so perceptive. *What is this craziness doing to our kids?*

I got Alex all cleaned up and then called the non-emergency number for the police. I explained that my husband was recovering from brain surgery and that he got into the car and went to a softball game that didn't exist. I explained that I was concerned because he hadn't driven in over a year. The female officer I spoke to took down my information: Eric's name, the license plate number, the make and model of our car, and said she would alert the officers. Within five or seven minutes after I called the police, Eric pulled into the driveway. He was gone nearly an hour. The scariest fifty minutes of my life.

I casually said, "Daddy's home," to the kids and they ran to the door, screaming, "Daddy! Daddy!"

I didn't say much to him right then. He said, "I drove all around and looked at all the fields, but I couldn't find anyone. I guess I am missing the game." I didn't say anything more to him about it.

We put the kids to bed and I made all my calls, calling Rick, Maureen, and everyone else, to let them know that Eric had arrived home safely. I also called the police department. They thanked me for the call and said that they would alert their officers. All my worrying about what the police were going to think or do and all they said was "Thank you."

Later, I asked Eric where he had driven and he named all the streets that confirmed he did drive to Lake Zurich. I tried to explain to Eric that he hadn't driven in over a year, but he got instantaneously aggravated. I dropped the subject with Eric, but one thing was clear. He could no longer have access to the car keys.

Masters Golf Tournament

AS YOU ALREADY KNOW, Eric was a sports fanatic. In the past, he had looked forward to watching the Masters Golf Tournament every year in April. When the Masters Golf Tournament was on, everything came to a screeching halt in our house. He never missed one hole of television coverage and would watch "Sports Center" highlights of the tournament each night.

In April of 2004, Eric was getting used to his travel routine to and from rehab at Anixter, as well as the daily routine during rehab. I remember being very excited because the Masters Golf Tournament was on and I knew how much Eric enjoyed it.

When Eric arrived home from rehab in April of 2004, I had all his favorite snacks ready and got him set up in his favorite chair. I turned The Masters on the TV and there he sat with his snacks, a drink, and his feet up on the Ottoman. What more could a guy ask for?

When I returned to the family room a little while later, I noticed Eric was watching some random channel with an infomercial on. I said, "Eric, the Masters is on. Don't you want to watch it?"

Eric said, "That's OK, I'm just going to watch this." My heart sank.

Looking back, I was probably so excited about Eric watching the Masters because I wanted the "new" Eric to be the same as the "old" Eric and he just wasn't. Far from it. And that was hard to admit.

Mother's Day 2004

MOTHER'S DAY WAS APPROACHING and the kids were very excited about gifts. I ordered a compact for my purse from a catalog, for Eric and the kids to give me for Mother's Day. On that day, I asked Eric to come in the office, so I could talk to him without the kids hearing. I told him I bought a gift for Mother's Day for myself from him and the kids to give me. I asked him to please call the kids into the office and tell them that they were going to give me the gift. I told him to hurry up before he forgot.

Eric called the kids into the office and told them. The kids were beaming. They gave me the gift and I acted very surprised, and everyone was happy. The funny thing was, when I was saying, "Thank you" to Eric and the kids, I could tell that Eric had already forgotten that I bought the gift myself. He actually looked proud, as if he had gone out and bought the gift.

Later that night, Alex said, "Mommy, Daddy is all better."

I was very confused. I asked Alex what she meant. She said, "Daddy drove to the store and bought you your Mother's Day gift, so he's all better."

"Oh," I said, amazed at the depth of Alex's thinking. Later, I told Alex that I had talked to Daddy and he told me that he ordered my gift from a catalog and it was sent through the mail. "Daddy still can't drive," I said, and I could see the disappointment wash over Alex's face.

May 21, 2004 – Can You Say, "Flop Sweat"?

WE TOOK THE KIDS to see the movie "Shrek 2" when it was newly released. We went to a theatre that had thirty different screens and stadium seating. Once we entered the theatre, we walked up about a quarter of the way, scooched down the aisle, passed a family of five, a father with his kids, and found four seats next to each other.

About half-way through the movie, I saw Eric doing his potty dance. I whispered, "Eric, go to the bathroom."

He said, "I will." He had waited until the last minute to go to the bathroom. I had no idea why.

A few minutes later, I told him, again, to go to the bathroom. I had to nag him every few minutes to remind him and he got very aggravated. Finally, he said, "OK!"

The movie was playing and the theatre was dark. Eric started to walk toward me, which was the long way. The exits were on his side, so coming my way made no sense. It would have been easier to go the other way and only pass the family of five. I told him to go the other way.

He turned around and walked out our aisle, but instead of going down the stairs he went up. He walked to the top of the theatre. He was way too far away for me to yell to him. I thought, "Where in the world is he going?"

I kept looking back and, sure enough, he went to the tippy-top of the theatre, where there was a red exit sign. I had no idea what was beyond the door. Eric disappeared beyond that door in a theatre complex that housed thirty movies, feared never to be seen again.

He was gone, and there I sat, our kids, happily watching "Shrek 2," unaware that their mother had broken into a flop sweat and their father may be on a milk carton soon.

I was panicked. My heart was racing. I thought he was going to wander down some hallway and never be able to find his way back to our theatre. It was hard enough when you have all your faculties, to find the people you were sitting with in the dark, upon returning from the bathroom, but add Eric's short-term memory issue and there could be a big problem.

My heart was racing as I kept looking back to the top of the theatre, sure that I was annoying the crap out of the people behind me. They were probably wondering what I was looking for. I started to think, "OK, the family of five... The husband looks decent. Maybe I could ask him to look after my kids, explain the situation etc., etc."

Then I looked over to my right and there was a mom and her daughter. I thought, "Well, I'm probably better off with a mother than a father."

Then I thought to myself, "Snap out of it! I can't ask a total stranger to watch my kids."

So I revised my thinking: I would have to get both kids out of their seats, and start searching the theatre for Eric. I was very worried. I continued to glance behind me to the back of the theatre.

I was just about to start gathering up the kids and our stuff and I looked again and here came Eric. He was back at the top door and walking down the stairs. He kept looking for us, but was watching the movie from the aisle as well. I knew he couldn't see or remember where we were, but he kept moving down the aisle step by step and then he'd watch the movie a little more. He finally got close enough and I was waving my arms to get his attention. *More fun for the folks sitting behind us.*

He didn't see us, so I finally just yelled "ERIC!" He scooched in, sat down, and watched the rest of the movie. I tried to get my breathing back to a normal pace and recover from my near heart attack. *Just a relaxing day at the movies.*

Life as "The Caregiver"

CAREGIVER. HAVE YOU EVER really thought about this word? I know I never did before Eric's brain tumor. At thirty-nine years old, a wife and mother of two, I never thought of being a caregiver to anyone else but my kids, especially not my forty-three year old, healthy husband.

Things change. *There's an understatement.* You just never know what tomorrow is going to bring. I didn't. Would you be ready? To say I was surprised or shocked didn't even scratch the surface. It felt like someone pulled the rug right out from underneath me and here I was, smack dab in the middle of a nightmare.

Eric's symptoms were very much like an Alzheimer's patient's symptoms. It is very difficult when the loved one you are caring for is unaware of his situation, while the caregiver is painfully aware of what has been lost and to what degree. The reminders come daily, hourly, minute-by-minute. Every time we repeat ourselves and every time we see the confused looks, we are reminded of the person we lost and the person who remains.

Eric's illness stirred up a huge range of emotions and feelings inside me. There were days I didn't even like Eric. OK, honestly, sometimes I couldn't stand his guts. He was selfish, crabby, and unappreciative. His personality had completely changed. He was no longer the man I married, the man I played golf with and traveled with and struggled through fertility issues with and adopted our two beautiful children with, the man who was my rock and on whom I counted; this was not him.

The new Eric was harsh, edgy, introverted and confused. I would never have married the post-brain-surgery Eric. My role slowly changed from being Eric's wife to being his caregiver. I lost any desire to be intimate with him. I directed his every move: when to eat, when to stop eating, when to drink and when to go to sleep. I even had to tell him when to wipe his nose.

Nothing like a snotty face to get me in the mood. Besides… sex? It had been a while. Would Eric even remember how to have sex? I suppose it was like riding a bike, huh?

On top of his undesirable personality, I had a horrifying realization one day that Eric had "the look." You know, "the look." The icky look that tells you something isn't quite right with someone. You could tell just by looking at him. I guess it was a shock to me because, early on, no one could tell anything was wrong with Eric unless they spoke to him for an extended period of time. It was only when he repeated himself or asked the same question did you get the feeling something was wrong. Now, all of a sudden, I saw that Eric had "the look" and it horrified me. How did that happen? When did that happen? *Oh God.*

I felt robbed. Your spouse is supposed to know everything about you. They know your hopes and fears. They know all the little details about you - how you take your coffee, your favorite food, your sleep habits, and your relationships with your family. They know with whom you get along and with whom you don't. They know how you argue and if you're crabby.

Your spouse is the person with whom you can communicate without speaking a word. You can finish each other's sentences. This is the person you have inside jokes and thermostat wars with. You make some of the biggest decisions of your life with this person. You purchase cars and homes with that person and if you have kids, your spouse is your teammate and partner in raising your kids.

I had all these things with Eric and now he didn't remember any of it. After Eric's surgery, he would always ask me if I wanted any coffee. I never drank coffee and still don't to this day. Eric used to know that and now he didn't. It made me sad and mad all at the same time. It was like being stabbed in the heart. Every time Eric asked me if I wanted coffee, it was like someone was twisting the knife, another reminder that Eric didn't know me anymore.

I felt mad that I wouldn't be able to socialize as a couple with people who did not know Eric before his brain tumor. He was different now. Strange. Quirky. Bizarre. People wouldn't understand what Eric had been through, how far he had come. They would just see the man talking back to the TV, spouting comments that made no sense, repeating the same questions over and over.

I feared I would be isolated socially because of Eric's condition, which was so ironic because pre-surgery Eric was the most social person you would ever want to meet.

I felt sadness. Sad for the kids. What would their memories of their dad be? Would they remember an angry, crabby daddy? I didn't want Alex and Tommy to "miss out" on a great relationship with their dad—their "old" dad, before surgery.

I felt pressure. Pressure because I was taking care of everyone and making every decision - decisions from what we were going to eat for every meal, to refinancing our mortgage, to choosing insurance coverage. If we went anywhere, it was because I planned it. I decided on what home improvements we needed. I made every decision.

Eric couldn't drive anymore and I remember thinking how nice it would just be to be able to be the passenger every once in a while. I needed a break.

There was one time, in the summer, when I just could not get out of bed. Eric was getting up pretty early and so was Tommy. We had the baby monitor in our room and sure enough, Tommy was calling, "Mommy, Mommy."

I said to Eric, "I can't move."

He said, "I'll get him."

I thought it was good that Eric took the initiative and said he'd get Tommy, even though I knew I should have gotten up. I told Eric, "Ok."

I heard Eric on the monitor in Tommy's room and he didn't say anything to Tommy. No warm greeting or good morning; he just took him out of the crib and brought him downstairs. Alex was still sleeping in her room.

I stayed in bed about five more minutes and thought, "What am I doing?" I knew it wasn't a good idea for Eric to be downstairs with Tommy all by himself.

When I went downstairs, Eric and Tommy were at the kitchen table. Eric had a bowl of cereal for himself and one for Tommy too, a ceramic bowl on the tray of Tommy's highchair. Tommy was 18 months old.

As I entered the kitchen, I heard Eric ask Tommy if he wanted any Sweet 'n Low on his cereal. Hmmm. This was when I realized I would always be the one to get up with the kids and there would be no more sleeping in.

I told Eric, "Tommy cannot have a ceramic bowl because he might push it right off the tray of his highchair." And "18-month old babies don't use Sweet 'n Low." Eric responded with a confused look, as if what I was saying made no sense to him. It wasn't registering.

I felt pressure because I was the one person keeping our family together. If I went down, the whole ship went down. It seemed that things built up over time and then the smallest issue would make me crumble.

One day, I got a notice in the mail that our minivan was due for the emissions test. Later the same day, the belt on my vacuum cleaner broke and I sat down and cried like a baby. Every responsibility was mine and the pressure was too much. I remember thinking to myself that I'd better be more careful crossing the street. I had to make sure Alex and Tommy didn't ever have to live without me.

I felt lonely. Although my husband was right there with me, I was unable to have any kind of meaningful conversation with him. I missed adult conversation and companionship. I was lonely because my partner, with whom I had planned to spend my life, was no longer there, and in his place was a guy who looked like Eric, but clearly wasn't.

Eric had been my rock. He was the first one I called with any problem or issue. He was so calm and approached everything so rationally and I missed him so much that I ached.

In December of 2004, a deadly Tsunami occurred in Southeast Asia that obliterated entire cities and communities. The devastation was horrifying. I couldn't help but see the parallels between the tsunami and the effects of Eric's illness. Eric's brain tumor blindsided us. Whoosh! All of a sudden we were knee deep in tumor, doctors and medical jargon. It obliterated our lives as we knew them. The tumor swept away my husband and his short-term memory and left us with a new "altered" Eric. Both events were horrible tragedies.

On a particularly tough day, I was sitting in an exam room with Eric during an appointment with his eye specialist and noticed the following poem on the doctor's wall. The poem was signed, "anonymous," but I later learned that the author is Mary Anne Radmacher. I felt like it was a message just for me at that moment on that particular day. Maybe it will help you, too.

<u>Live With Intention</u>
Walk to the edge
Listen hard
Practice wellness
Play with abandon
Laugh
Choose With No Regret
Continue to learn
Appreciate your friends
Do what you love
Live as if this is all there is.

Gutter Cleaning - Friday, May 28, 2004

IT WAS FRIDAY OF MEMORIAL DAY weekend. Eric arrived home from rehab and everything seemed to be fine. We needed to clean our gutters, a very overdue project, which was obvious by the science experiments growing in the full length of our gutters. This was not a fun project to do under normal circumstances, but even less fun with my brain-injured spouse.

Since the brain tumor, I was the one who had to go up the ladder and onto the roof. I climbed the ladder with my bucket, got on the roof, and started scooping the putrid smelling sludge out of the gutters. My garden glove-covered hand was soaked after the first scoop... lovely.

As I scooped the sludge into the bucket, Eric started to talk incessantly, nonsensical, musical phrases, borderline taunting me. "Wendy you're doing a great job." (dripping with sarcasm) "Keep up the good work. Does that stuff really smell? That must be pretty nasty. I'm glad I'm not up there scooping up that stuff." *Ok, I am being heckled by my husband as I clean the fricking gutters.* I gritted my teeth and just tried to clean as fast as I could.

When I finished the perimeter of the garage, we had to move the extension ladder along the rest of the house. This nearly sent us to divorce court! Eric insisted he could do it himself. I watched him hoist the extension ladder vertically, twenty-eight feet in the air, swaying to and fro. I was sure he was going to swing it right into one of our windows, or the momentum would overpower him and the ladder would fall on our minivan.

As he struggled to control the ladder, I approached to help. I got on one side and told Eric to grab the other, and explained how we would both move the ladder to the correct position. The mocking continued.

He had absolutely no judgment, crookedly positioning the ladder against the house. After a lot of arguing with each other, the gutter cleaning continued and so did the heckling. *(I must admit the urge to scoop up the sludge and drop it on Eric's head was strong, but you'll be happy to know that I fought it.)* When I got down off the roof, my neighbor friends were out and I remember approaching them and saying something along the lines of, "I hate my husband." *Not my proudest moment.*

I knew that if Eric had been aware of what was happening to him and how he was behaving, he would be absolutely mortified. He certainly didn't want to be this way. On the days when I just couldn't stand his guts, I reminded myself that it was not his fault and the "old" Eric would never have behaved this way.

For a while after this gutter-cleaning nightmare, I hired a guy who came and cleaned our gutters. Eventually, we had new gutters put on the house that came with gutter guards. Let me tell you, it is worth every penny!

In The Mood...Out of the Mood

THE QUESTION ABOUT INTIMACY in the midst of all this craziness has come up again and again. The reality was that Eric's sexual function had decreased to a very diminished capacity. Because of the brain injury, the necessary messages were not making it from his brain to where they needed to go, if you catch my drift.

As we all know from those annoying commercials, there is also a "magic pill" for this issue. Yipeee! The pills are "effective" for 24 to 36 hours from the time they are taken. This set off a whole new set of complicated scenarios.

Here I was with a husband who had no short-term memory and no self-awareness as to what had happened to him. Now, on those rare instances when I was feeling amorous toward him, I would have to give him a pill and explain what it was for, planning for future "activities." *Can you just imagine his confusion when I launched into that explanation!*

So many times, I'd give him a pill in anticipation of some time together. Then, through the course of the day, he would have an episode of some kind, or have a softball game that I couldn't talk him out of, or he'd argue with me about whether I had fed him or not, and any trace of loving feelings I had toward him went right down the drain.

That whole activity just became one more thing I had to control. The last thing I needed, or wanted, was another responsibility, especially for something like that.

I can't tell you how many of those little blue pills went to waste...

Anixter evaluation form

IN JUNE OF 2004, THREE MONTHS after starting the Anixter program, Eric had his first evaluation. All of Eric's therapists attended the meeting, along with our caseworker from the department of rehabilitation services, and me. Each therapist gave a verbal report of what they were working on with Eric and set goals to complete before the next evaluation period. At the end, they gave Eric a feedback form to fill out and return. The form had six questions.

> **Q1.** What goals do you believe are most important at this time?
> **Eric's answer:** 1. Improve memory function 2. Improve reasoning skills
> **Q2.** What things do you find difficult to do?
> **Eric's answer:** Improve my memory function
> **Q3.** What things do you do well?
> **Eric's answer:** Reasoning skills, daily living skills, physical condition
> **Q4.** What do you like about the program?
> **Eric's answer:** It is an honest program
> **Q5.** What don't you like about the program?
> **Eric's answer:** A little too large of a program
> **Q6.** What would you like to see changed?
> **Eric's answer:** A bit smaller clientele
> **Participants Comments:**
> **Eric wrote:** This program has significantly assisted me in recovering from my heart attack.

His heart attack? Oh my God. This was a perfect example of how unaware Eric was of what had happened to him. He also frequently made comments that he had terrible pain in his feet and I'd ask him why he thought that was and he said because of all the foot surgery he had. *You guessed it; he never ever had foot surgery.*

Talking to Eric About Reality

IN JUNE OF 2004, NO MATTER HOW HARD I tried to distract him, softball was still my biggest issue. I tried a new approach and talked to Eric about his situation when I picked him up from the train station after rehab.

I reminded Eric that he was just getting in from downtown, where he attended rehab that was part of his recovery from brain surgery. I said that he was having trouble recognizing what had happened to him and that he was sometimes confused about reality.

I told him that he thought he played softball, but in reality, he didn't. Although he thought he had games everyday, he really didn't.

I let him know that there was nothing I wanted more than for him to get better, but it wasn't going to happen until he opened up his mind and believed the things I was telling him.

I told him I knew that things seemed very real, but they weren't and I didn't want to just humor him and tell him what he wanted to hear. I told Eric he needed to trust me and believe me.

The whole tone of the conversation was very serious. He really seemed to be taking it all in. Unfortunately, after we arrived home Eric went straight for the address book and started calling around to find out where the game was. He didn't remember our conversation.

The Captain Gets a Little Reprieve...

Thursday Nights Out – June 2004

AFTER ERIC WAS HOME ABOUT A YEAR, I finally realized that I had to get out a little or I'd go crazy. As many people were telling me, if I went down, the whole ship would go down. *How's that for pressure?*

I decided I would finally join the choir at church, which was something I had wanted to do for quite a while. I had to ask people to be with Eric and the kids. Thanks to my brother, Eric's cousins and our friends, I was able to go to choir practice once a week.

In the beginning, I felt sorry for Eric and thought maybe he'd feel embarrassed that someone had to come and sit with him. To soften the blow I'd say, "Oh look, so and so stopped by to visit (wink, wink), but I'm on my way to choir practice, so enjoy visiting."

After several months I would say, "So and so is coming to help you watch the kids while I go to choir practice." Eric would never say a word. He would never question why someone else would need to come and help him babysit his own kids.

When people did come over, Eric wouldn't converse at all. He'd just stare a hole through the TV, only speaking when spoken to.

As we had discovered with the train, Eric was capable of new learning with a lot of repetition. After about a year of having someone sit with him on Thursday nights, Eric had learned the routine of putting the kids to bed.

One time, I told him someone was coming to help him watch the kids while I went to choir practice and Eric asked, "Do I need help?" Wow. It blew me away. It was the first time he ever had a response on this subject. I sloughed it off and told him that I wouldn't do that to him—have him watch the kids all on his own. He never protested.

Eric had gotten to the point where he would change Tommy's diaper and put the kids to bed on his own without prompting.

I decided to let Eric stay with the kids alone while I went to choir practice. By this time, Alex was 5 ½ years old and Tommy was

3 ½. Thank goodness for cell phones. I would get the kids ready for bed before I left and leave seven or eight notes around the house that contained the following message:

Eric,

I am at choir practice. Please put the kids to bed at 8:00 p.m. I will be home around 9:30 p.m. I will call you and check in. If you need to contact me, call my cell at (847)xxx-xxxx.

Love,
Wendy

I would purposely call from choir practice when it was time for Eric to put the kids to bed and tell him to tuck them in. I'd call 30 minutes later to make sure he did.

The phone calls were a little unnerving. A typical phone conversation went like this:

Me: Hi honey, it's me.

Eric: Where are you?

Me: Do you see the note right next to your chair?

(I'd hear the crumpling of paper)

Eric: Oh yeah, you're at choir.

Me: How are the kids?

Eric: I don't know, they're not down here.

Me: When I called 30 minutes ago you were going to put them to bed. Can you walk upstairs and check on them while I'm still on the phone?

He would check and he'd confirm that the kids were sleeping in their beds.

Occasionally I'd come home and the kids would be up, watching TV with Eric. They must have come back downstairs and Eric let them stay up. I was usually home by 9:30 p.m. from choir and figured if the kids were up late every now and then, relatively speaking, it wasn't a big deal.

In addition to choir practice once a week, I was able to play Bunco once a month with the neighborhood moms and Eric was able to stay with the kids. I used all the same strategies of leaving notes and calling home several times a night to check in. Almost every time I'd call home, Eric would ask where I was, even though I had just called an hour before and the reminder notes were all over the house. In both cases, I was never farther away than a five-minute drive.

Over the next few years, as the kids got older, they realized they could manipulate the situation. We had an agreement that they could watch the reality TV show, "Survivor" and go to bed when it was over.

Eric would tell them it was time for bed at 8:00, but Alex would ask to watch one more show and Eric always said, "Yes."

When I'd call to make sure they were in bed, Eric would say, "No, the kids are right here."

Then I would speak with Alex and scold her for not going to bed when she was supposed to. "It's wrong to ask Daddy for things, knowing he'll say, 'Yes,' when you know it's not right." Looking back, it was probably too much responsibility to put on her.

Eric never told them, "No" about anything. He didn't have the awareness to know that the kids needed their sleep or that giving endless snacks wasn't healthy.

When solicitors called on the phone, Eric usually made appointments for them to come and sell us windows, aluminum siding or "whatever." On several occasions, Alex told me the next morning that "Daddy talked on the phone to someone for a long time last night." Thank goodness for caller ID and The Do Not Call List. *Can you imagine his answers to some of the people who called for surveys?!*

In spite of it all, and most importantly, getting out saved my sanity.

"This is my favorite picture of Eric and Tommy. It was taken 17 months after surgery.

Mr. Cranky Conductor

IN AUGUST OF 2004, I WAS ON THE PHONE with Eric as he waited at the Clybourne train platform for the train home. Eric heard an overhead announcement that the track had changed for the train that was due in. I overheard Eric tell someone else standing there that the track had changed. I was very impressed, especially because, another time, he missed an announcement about a track change and had to wait an hour for the next train.

This time, because I wasn't 100% sure that Eric got to the correct track as per the announcement, I told Eric to confirm with the conductor that the train stopped in Palatine. I was still on the cell phone and heard Eric's conversation with the conductor. "Does this train stop at Palatine?" Eric asked.

The conductor replied with a mean, yelling tone, as if Eric were a kid being punished. "You ask me that everyday. Don't your wife and kids pick you up everyday in Palatine?"

Eric was a better person than I would have been, simply replying, "Thank you very much" in a quiet tone.

When Eric found a seat on the train and continued to talk to me on the cell phone, I told him how angry I was with the conductor's tone and attitude and asked him why he didn't say anything? Eric said, "It's no big deal."

I hung up after telling Eric I would be there when he arrived at the station. I was furious with that conductor and as every minute passed, I got angrier.

I was standing on the platform when Eric's train arrived and when the conductor stepped off the train, I tapped him firmly on the shoulder. "Excuse me sir. Do you see this man right here? (gesturing to Eric) He is my husband. The reason he asks you everyday if the train stops at Palatine is because he suffered a brain injury and has no memory."

The conductor asked me, "Did he call you and tell you about our conversation?" *The nerve of this guy.*

I said, "No, I was on the cell phone with him and heard the entire thing with my own ears. So the next time he asks you if the train stops in Palatine, just say, 'Yes,' because that's your job."

The conductor, again with a defiant tone said, "He asks me the same question everyday."

I told him, "He asks me the same questions everyday too. He has no memory." My tone was nothing short of ticked off.

The conductor stammered and said, "Oh…well… Thanks for telling me."

I trembled with anger for about 30 minutes after this incident. First of all, I would think that if someone asked you the same question everyday, you would assume something wasn't quite right with that person. Maybe the conductor felt Eric was trying to harass him or something, but the bottom line was that it was his job to answer the passengers' questions and all it takes is one word… "Yes."

This incident made me realize Eric's vulnerability. The fact that this man treated Eric with such disrespect worried me. I felt nervous and upset that Eric either couldn't or didn't know to defend himself in a situation like that.

More Telephone Adventures

IT WAS THE SUMMER OF 2004 and Eric was still obsessed with two things: softball and work.

I would cringe when he'd call his old company. Eric always thought people were lying when they told him he didn't work at that company any longer. He would say, "Why are you saying this to me? You know I work there."

It was very sad. I started making Eric keep a phone log as he sat and made calls. If he called Janet at his old office, I made him write her name down and what time he called. I did the same for his softball calls. When he would go to repeat a call to the same person, I'd point out on the log that he already talked to that person.

Sometimes he would acknowledge that he called the person, but they weren't available so he had to call again. I had to add a section to the call log for call content. This didn't eliminate the calling, but it did cut down on the number of times he called each person.

I was trying to protect him from embarrassing himself. If Eric were aware that he was calling his old company, he would have been mortified.

In August of 2004, when we returned from picking up Eric at the train, all the neighborhood kids were outside playing, so of course our kids wanted to play, too. I knew that if I left Eric alone in the house, he would dial Siberia to find out what time the game was. The phone bill was getting brutal, but it was such a nice day and I didn't feel like being the phone monitor today. He could call the fricking White House for all I cared, I just wanted to enjoy the nice weather.

I got Eric settled in his chair, turned on ESPN and got him a drink. He seemed to be content. He didn't even mention softball. I told him I was going out on the driveway with the kids for a while.

Periodically, I went in to check on Eric. When the light under the kitchen cabinet was on, that was a sign that Eric was on the phone. The first few times I checked on him, everything looked fine. He was still sitting in his chair watching TV. The final time I checked, the light under the kitchen cabinet was on and the phone was sitting on the table next to Eric's chair. I asked him if anyone called or if he called anyone and he said no. I knew it wasn't true, not that he was lying, he just didn't remember.

I cleaned up outside, brought the kids in and got ready for dinner. I noticed our calendar was on the counter and Eric wrote down "Window Company, 1:30 p.m." on Friday of the following week. The phone call Eric answered was a solicitor and Eric agreed to an appointment. I asked Eric why he made the appointment and he said, "Because the guy wanted to come by." A solicitor's dream! I told Eric we didn't need windows and he just shrugged his shoulders.

The following week, while my mom was in town and I was out running errands, she informed me that the window company called to confirm their appointment and she cancelled it.

Oh Yes... and Patience

MOST OF THE TIME, I WAS VERY PATIENT with Eric... and trust me, there is no one more surprised than me. I am the same person who didn't want to wait three days for my bathroom wallpaper, so I settled for an in-stock pattern and took it home immediately. Patience was never my strong suit. With Eric, I amazed myself how many times I could answer the same question, or repeat directions over and over without going berserk.

Now, before you heap on the accolades, let me tell you, I had my moments when I let loose and screamed and hollered in frustration, and could be very cruel and sarcastic. I always felt horrible after one of my fits. Although Eric wasn't able to remember my meltdowns after a few minutes, I did, and it made me feel terribly guilty.

On good days, when my patience seemed endless, I thought to myself, "The poor guy. He doesn't want to be like this. If he knew, he'd be mortified." This was all true.

On my not-so-good days, when I couldn't muster a drop of patience, I thought to myself, "Well... I am the one who has to deal with this everyday, 24/7. I'm losing my mind and I just want my husband back!"

Thank You Hollywood!

BY SEPTEMBER OF 2004, I thought I was going crazy with Eric calling his old office and having softball every night. I stole an idea from a movie that came out earlier in the year called "50 First Dates," starring Drew Barrymore and Adam Sandler. Drew's character suffered from short-term memory loss. She could retain her memory during the day, but once she slept and woke up the next day, her memory was gone again. Adam Sandler's character made a videotape that she could watch everyday to tell her what was going on in her life.

At least Drew's character could retain her memory for a full day. Eric couldn't remember anything from five minutes ago. I made a tape for Eric and I recorded an opening message to him telling him what the tape was all about. I answered some of his frequently asked questions and explained his current situation, including the fact that he thought he played softball but he didn't. Then I taped the kids just saying hi to Eric.

I then called our friends, Rick and Don. They were golf buddies of Eric's, although Eric thought they played softball together. I had them come over and taped each one of them, separately talking into the camera to Eric. They each had a similar message, starting out by telling Eric what month and year it was and then explaining to Eric that he had brain surgery and as a result, he was a little confused about what was happening in his life.

I not only thought this tape would be a good tool for both of us, but I also thought it would be good for Eric to hear this information from someone other than me. I had been telling him these things everyday. Maybe hearing it from someone else would make a bigger impact.

Don and Rick told Eric he was not working right now, but rather attending rehab in order to get better from his brain surgery. They told him that they were golf buddies and explained that he was confused and thought they played softball, which, they pointed out, was not true. They each told Eric to believe me when I told him something because what I said was the truth and I was just trying to help him. Each video lasted about three to four minutes, but contained all the information I needed Eric to hear.

Then I sent the tape to Eric's friend in Virginia and he also recorded a three to four minute message to Eric.

Eric Schmude explained to Eric that although they did play softball when they were younger, they hadn't played together in over 20 years. Eric Schmude also ended his recording by telling Eric to believe me when I told him things because I was trying very hard to help him.

Eric Schmude then mailed the tape to our friend D.R. in Pittsburgh and D.R. recorded a similar message. When D.R. mailed the tape back to me, I met with Eric's work colleague, Janet, and she was nice enough to record a message to Eric, too. She chronicled the timeline outlining when Eric left the company and that he hadn't worked there for quite a while. She told Eric that he was attending rehab to recover from his brain surgery.

The finished product was a 25-minute videotape that I could show Eric to help him understand that he no longer played softball or worked for the company that he kept calling every day.

It didn't take long to test the videotape. The day after I finished recording Janet's portion of the tape, Eric came home from rehab and grabbed the address book to start making his calls. He was about to call Eric Schmude in Virginia and I asked him, "Are you calling Eric Schmude about softball tonight?"

He said, "Yes." I asked him if Rick and Don were on the team too and Eric said, "Yes."

I said, "Your friends left you a message about it on a video. Come watch it with me in the family room."

I sat Eric down in his chair, turned on the TV, and I pressed the play button on the video recorder to start the tape. First I appeared on the screen. I watched Eric watch me. No reaction. Then he watched the kids and smiled. He watched the rest of the tape and had no reaction.

When it was over I asked him what he thought. He said, "So they're saying I haven't worked in 1 ½ years?"

I said, "Right."

Eric's nose crinkled and he looked like he was thinking really hard. Most importantly, he didn't say another word. He grabbed the TV remote, turned on "Jeopardy," and never said a word about work or softball the rest of the night. *Can you believe it?*

For the next two months it was the same scenario each day. Eric would come home from rehab, get the address book out, I'd have him watch the videotape and one of three things would happen; 1) He'd watch the whole tape and wouldn't say a word, 2) He'd ask a few questions and that would be it or 3) He'd fall asleep watching the tape. No matter which of the three scenarios happened, that was the end of softball for the rest of that day.

The tape worked for two months. September and October of 2004 were the most peaceful two months of the whole ordeal. One day in November, Eric came home from rehab and got the address book out and I said, "Are you going to start calling around about softball?"

Eric answered in an agitated tone," Yes, and don't try and show me that videotape because I don't want to see it and I do have softball." *The party's over.*

I don't know what was suddenly different, but whatever it was about the tape that satisfied Eric the previous two months, wore off. *Damn.*

I thought it was interesting that he remembered the video. Maybe it took that many repeat viewings to seal it in his memory. Whatever it was, the softball nightmare continued. I even took Eric to a few sessions of hypnosis to see if we could get rid of his obsession, but that didn't work either.

A Warm Pizza Man on a Cold Day

ON A FREEZING COLD DAY in the dead of winter, Eric got lost walking to the train platform to catch the train home after rehab. I called him on the cell phone as I always did, and he told me nothing looked familiar and named streets I hadn't heard of before.

I told him to look around and tell me if there were any stores he could see. He walked for a while and then said there was a pizza place up near the corner. Giving one direction at a time, I told him to go inside the pizza place. When he got inside, I asked him if there was someone working at the counter. He said, "Yes."

Then I asked Eric to hand his cell phone to the person working behind the counter so I could talk to them. He didn't want to do that. I think, somewhere deep-down, he knew he should be able to handle things himself, even though he struggled. He wouldn't hand his cell phone to the guy, so I told Eric to tell the guy he needed directions to the Clybourne train platform.

I heard the man giving directions, but I couldn't hear them very well. I heard Eric say, "Thanks." And out the door he went. The next thing I heard was the man calling after Eric and telling him he turned the wrong way when he left the restaurant.

I was very concerned now and Eric must have heard it in my voice because I demanded that he hand his cell phone to the man so I could talk with him. This time, Eric handed him the phone.

I explained to the man that Eric was my husband and that he had a brain injury and got turned around walking to the train platform. I asked him to please repeat the directions to me so I could direct Eric from the cell phone.

The man said, "Listen, it's really cold outside. How about if I drive your husband to the train platform?"

I couldn't believe it. Here is this total stranger making such a nice offer. I have to admit that I was a little nervous about it, but I accepted his offer.

I got back on the cell phone with Eric and told him to get in the car with the man and he would drive him to the train. I was on the phone with Eric the whole time and heard the man tell Eric that they had arrived and he pointed out the set of stairs Eric had to walk up. I asked Eric to hand his cell phone to the man and I thanked him profusely.

Eric got on the train and made it home.

I had so many emotions as a result of this situation. I was grateful that the man, a total stranger, was so kind to Eric and did such a wonderful deed. I was also scared because Eric had gotten lost. It was very cold that day.

What if I hadn't been able to reach him on the cell phone and he just kept wandering in the cold? It was too scary to think about.

I realized I could play the "What if?" game all day long. It didn't happen; the man was incredibly nice and helped Eric. That's what I had to focus on and be grateful for that day.

Coping: Sense of Humor — Essential

SOME OF THE QUESTIONS I got frequently are, "How do you do it?" "How do you cope?" "How do you deal with everything that has happened?"

One of the ways I coped was I engaged in some major stress eating. It usually took place at night, after I had put the kids to bed and had given Eric his nighttime medications. I sat in my chair, put my feet up on my ottoman, turned on the TV and ate.

My food of choice was usually a can of Pillsbury frosting. *(French vanilla flavor, if you're wondering.)* It was just me, a spoon, and the frosting. True nirvana. I remember one time, our daughter, Alex, went to throw something in the garbage, saw an empty can of frosting and asked, "Did we have a cake I didn't know about?" *Talk about a shame spiral.*

Giant Hershey Bars and Fannie May milk chocolate vanilla butter creams were also in my top five stress-eating food choices. But I would have to say the thing that helped me cope the most was the gift I received from my parents—my sense of humor.

My dad had a very dry sense of humor. He was a very quiet man of few words. When he made a joke, if you didn't catch it, he didn't repeat it. Unlike my dad, if I make a joke and someone doesn't hear it, I will repeat it until they do.

My mom had the greatest sense of humor of anyone I knew. Her humor was more on the silly side - plays on words, gag jokes, visuals. She was the person I laughed the most with in my life. It's quite a gift, the ability to see the humor in things, but if you knew the major heartache my mom had to overcome in her life (twice widowed and the loss of her 18-year-old daughter to a car accident) you could see that she was a truly amazing person.

I could never claim to have had anything but a wonderful life, but I've had my share of turmoil and my sense of humor always helped me through. Never did I need it more than during the years when my life as I knew it came crashing in around me.

Start of Positive Changes

EVEN THOUGH ERIC STILL demonstrated wacky behavior, couldn't remember five minutes ago, and still obsessed about softball daily, there were also positive changes happening. Eric could perform all of his activities of daily living on his own and he was much more interactive and loving toward the kids. He would pour them drinks and get them snacks and they'd sit on his lap and watch TV.

Eric would clear the table after meals and load and unload the dishwasher. If I was folding laundry, he would come over and help me without me asking. I had a lot of friends say their husbands didn't do that stuff and they never had a brain tumor! Eric demonstrated new learning by taking the train to and from Anixter for rehab and he was staying with the kids alone while I went to choir practice.

For Mother's Day 2005, Eric was able to write in a card for his mom, unlike the previous years, when he couldn't write in a straight line or focus on what to write.

I had to keep focusing on these positive changes because the challenges just kept coming quickly and furiously.

Losing Eric at the Mall

I AM IN THE STAGE OF MY LIFE where I have begun misplacing things. Now more than ever, I always seem to be looking for something. I am also doing the thing where you enter a room and just stand there and stare because you can't remember why you went in the room. *Humor me and tell me you do it too.*

My mother-in-law says I do this because I have so many thoughts running through my head at once and I am always multi-tasking. I'm going with her explanation, whether it's true or not, because it makes me feel better.

Since Eric's surgery, not just I, but various family members, have lost Eric on a number of occasions. Can you imagine losing a 6'2", 250 lb. man? Now that's an accomplishment. Anyone can lose their keys, but a husband?

The first time we lost Eric was during a shopping trip to the mall. Eric's mom was in town and our babysitter, Dana, stayed with the kids while the three of us went shopping.

As we drove the 15 minutes to the mall, Eric kept looking at the empty car seat in the van, and then he'd ask, "Where's Alex?"

"She's at home with the babysitter," was our consistent reply, which satisfied Eric for five minutes, until he asked again.

We entered the mall and shopped in the first store for a while. Then, as we walked through the mall toward Marshall Fields, Eric again panicked, looking all over, thinking we lost Alex. This time our explanation didn't convince Eric because he was sure Alex had been right there with us. It seemed a cruel joke that no matter how incorrect or bizarre they were, Eric's thoughts were very, very real to him.

I called home on my cell phone and asked Dana to put Alex on the phone. Eric asked Alex what she was doing and if she was having fun. When he hung up the phone he shrugged his shoulders in confusion.

We arrived at Marshall Field's and continued shopping. I picked several items to try on and left Eric with his mom while I went into the dressing room. Nothing thrilled me, so I went out and found Eric's mom. Right away I got nervous because Eric was not with her.

"Where's Eric?" I asked her.

"I sat him down on a chair by the dressing rooms," she replied.

At this point we were both white as ghosts because the chair was empty. My eyes immediately scanned the store. It was overwhelming how huge the store appeared to me at that moment. At one end were the exit doors to the parking garage, and at the other end, closest to us, was the exit into the mall.

I sent Eric's mom in one direction and I went the other. I was yelling Eric's name really loudly, frantically searching every aisle. "Eric, Eric, Eric." I'm sure anyone who saw me assumed I had lost my child.

My heart was pounding out of my chest and I was racking my brain trying to remember what Eric was wearing, already conducting the police interview in my head. I'm sure only about four minutes had passed, but it seemed like forever, when I finally spotted Eric, way at the other end of the store toward the parking garage exits.

When I got to Eric the first thing he said to me was, "I can't find Alex."

I imagined that while Eric was sitting in the chair, the thought must have crossed his mind that Alex was missing, and he started walking around the store looking for her.

I explained to Eric again that Alex was at home with Dana. He didn't remember talking to her on the cell phone earlier. I told Eric how scared we were because we thought we had lost him. He shrugged the comment off with a confused look.

I walked with Eric to the other side of the store, where we met up with his mother. She breathed a huge sigh of relief when she saw him.

After arriving home and paying the babysitter, Eric seemed perfectly content, but I was still shaken. The fear coursing through my veins when I was searching for Eric was sobering. Losing Eric brought so many unanswered questions to the surface about Eric's ability to take care of himself. Would he know how to find his way back home if he needed to? Would he know how to call home? Because his mind played tricks on him with innumerable random thoughts, he was very vulnerable.

Within minutes of Eric's head hitting his pillow he was calmly snoring. I couldn't seem to get the racing thoughts of our mall adventure out of my head, which was ironic because Eric didn't even remember going to the mall that day.

Losing Eric At Home

YES, I KNOW, WHEN DOES the craziness end, right? It's true—
we lost Eric in our own house, too. All of our cousins were in town,
staying just across town at their sister, Mary's house. Eric's parents
were in town, staying with us. We decided to spend a day downtown
at the aquarium.

Then Eric's mom offered to watch Eric and the kids downtown
if I wanted a day at home alone. I accepted. It was nice to have a whole
day to myself at home, just to read or do whatever I wanted. I have to
admit it seemed strange.

Later, when everyone returned from a fun day at the aquarium,
the kids were tired and went to bed, and all the cousins went back to
Mary's house, except for Kathleen. She came back to our house to
have a piece of blueberry pie before she went back to her sister's for the
night. *I, for one, don't feel you should ever mess up a pie by putting fruit in
it, but that's another book.*

Grandpa, Eric, and Kathleen sat down for a piece of pie. I told
Grandpa that he was in charge of getting Eric upstairs to our bedroom
when it was bedtime, and I said good night to everyone.

About one hour later, there was a knock at our bedroom door.
When I opened it up, it was Grandpa standing there and asking if I
knew where Eric was. I said "No, I put you in charge of him."

Grandpa said that Kathleen left after they had pie, and she went
back to Mary's. He went outside to smoke a cigarette and when he
came back inside, Eric wasn't in the kitchen anymore.

I was instantly nervous. I went downstairs with Grandpa and
we looked for Eric. We couldn't find him anywhere. He wasn't in the
living room, dining room, kitchen, family room, or bathroom. I went
down in the basement and checked, but he wasn't there either.

I was starting to panic. Where in the world could he have gone?
He had never wandered out the front door before. What if he was
outside somewhere? *There's that "What if..." thing again.*

I went out in the garage and there he was. Every door in the van was open and Eric was searching under the seats for something. I said, "Eric, I've been looking all over for you. What are you doing out here?"

"I'm looking for the blueberry pie."

Doesn't everyone hide their blueberry pie under the seats of their vehicle?

"Eric, you already had a piece of pie with your dad and Kathleen."

"No, I did not."

I convinced Eric to come into the house. The three plates from blueberry pie were sitting in the sink. "Eric, look! Here are the three plates still in the sink. One was yours, one was your dad's, and one was Kathleen's. See, you had blueberry pie already."

Again he replied, "No I did not have pie," in a very aggravated tone.

I said, "Let's call Kathleen. She's over at Mary's. She'll tell you that you ate pie together."

I called over to Mary's and Eric got on the phone with Kathleen. I heard Eric say, "Yes, I know."

He turned to me and said "See. I did have pie tonight."

I almost blew my stack. I said, "I know! That's what I've been saying all along. But you insisted that you did not have any pie tonight and that's why we called Kathleen."

Eric said, "Yes I did have pie. I knew I was right." *Ahhhh!*

This is when it dawned on me that I would never win another argument with Eric again. *Don't worry. I eventually stopped trying.*

His memory was so damaged that he couldn't even keep track of what argument he was making. It was an exciting end to a relaxing day. I could have done with a little less excitement.

I Hate the Mall

THE DAY BEFORE THANKSGIVING, we were shopping for shoes for both our kids and as much as I hated the idea, we had to go to the mall because I had no luck anywhere else. I thought, "How busy could it be?" Besides, the big shopping day is always the day <u>after</u> Thanksgiving, right? *Yeah, right.*

We got to the mall and tried several stores close to Nordstrom's where we had parked, but, no luck. Begrudgingly, we ventured to the middle of the mall where I knew there was a children's shoe store. Apparently, nobody got the memo that the day after Thanksgiving was the busiest day. The mall was packed.

As we walked the upper level of the mall, Tommy saw Santa's Play Land and asked, "Can we go down and play at the play land?"

I said, "No. We're shopping for shoes and then going straight home."

When we got to the children's shoe store in the main corridor of the mall, the kids took off their coats and went straight to the play area in the corner of the store. Eric sat on the couch, while I picked out two pairs of shoes and the saleswoman went in the back to retrieve the sizes we needed.

Suddenly, Eric stood up and said, "I have to go to the bathroom, I'll be right back," and he stepped out into the main corridor of the mall.

I yelled, "Eric, no! Wait for us!" And off he went.

As I watched him walk down the busy mall aisle, I was in temporary shock. I knew he wasn't going to remember what store we were in. This was the problem. He was unaware of his memory deficit and thought he was fine. He really believed he'd just meet us back there. But, in reality, he couldn't remember and had absolutely no self-awareness. Panic stricken, I watched him walk away. He was tall, so I could see him for a minute. But just like you see in the movies, he got swallowed up by the crowd and I couldn't see him anymore.

I grabbed the kids and their jackets, and we ran out of the shoe store. I was holding the kids hands and told them, "We're running to find Daddy."

As we approached the end of the corridor and the JCPenney store, I scanned the big open area, back and forth. I didn't see him. The mall was very crowded and he was nowhere to be found, vanished.

I tried to think as he would. He had to go to the bathroom. Would he go into one of the many stores we passed and ask them if they had a bathroom? I looked down to the lower level and saw a long hallway with a restroom sign. Would Eric know to go downstairs to look for a bathroom? Did he see the sign? How the heck did I know?

The kids and I were standing there and I told them to look around for Daddy. I was nervous and scared. The mall didn't have a speaker system for announcements, so how the heck would I find him? Did he walk outside the mall? Should I walk downstairs to that restroom and see if he was there? But if I did, I wouldn't be able to see this open area of the mall to see if Eric walked by.

Now Alex was scared and started to cry. "I miss Daddy. Where's Daddy?" She kept repeating.

I was clearly doing a bad job of acting calm. Tommy said, "When we find Daddy, can we go to the play land?" The kid had a one-track mind.

"We'll talk about it later," I snapped.

Ten minutes had passed since Eric walked away. I decided to go downstairs to the restroom and see if he was there. I asked a man who was waiting with his wife and infant baby if he could please check in the men's room and see if anyone named Eric was inside. He checked and told me no one was in there. *Crap.*

We ran down the long hallway, went to the upper level, and returned to the open area in front of JCPenney. Scan...scan...scan. Nothing. Then I thought we would run back to the shoe store, just in case by some miracle of miracles, Eric did remember and went back there. I was running, holding hands with both kids who were practically airborne and I asked the lady at the shoe store if my husband, a man in a leather jacket, came in here looking for his family. She said, "No."

We ran back down to the area outside JCPenney and kept looking. At this point, I was convinced I would have to go to customer service, tell them what happened and see if they could help. I was sure some kids have been lost in the mall. They must have some kind of plan. The only difference was Eric was a grown man who thought he knew what was going on. He probably didn't think he was lost and wouldn't ask for help as a child might.

It was now 25 minutes since Eric bolted. As I scanned the area, I couldn't believe my eyes. There was Eric walking across the open area of JCPenney, walking from one side of the store to the other. If I hadn't seen him at that very moment, he would have walked to the other side of the store and been out of sight.

From the depth of my gut I yelled, "Eric!" and he stopped. He heard me, but couldn't see me. I kept yelling his name as I walked toward him, and he finally saw me.

I asked, "Were you looking for us?"

He said, "Yes."

I told him (*trying not to sound like a frazzled lunatic*), "We've been looking for you for twenty-five minutes. We even went back to the shoe store in case you went back there."

I asked him if he went to the bathroom and he said, "Yes."

Then I asked, "If we hadn't found you right then, how would you have found us?" He said he would have looked for us in the shoe store.

I said, "Oh. What shoe store were we in?"

He said, "The one in JCPenney." *Mind you we were standing under the enormous JCPenney sign having this conversation.*

My aggravation level skyrocketed. I said, "No Eric, we were at a different shoe store way down in the middle of the mall." Again, no reaction from Eric.

Trying to see if he had any common sense or reasoning skills to deal with this situation, I asked, "If you weren't able to find us what would you have done?"

"I would have gone to the car and met you there."

I asked, "Where did we park?" *I'll give you one guess what his answer was.*

"Outside JCPenney," Eric said calmly.

I'm glad he could be so calm. He had no idea how terrifying this situation was.

How in the world would I have found him? Where would he have wandered? Would he have had the sense to call me? We'll never know, but this trip to the mall was way too stressful for me. I used to scoff at the moms you would see in the mall with leashes on their children. That's what I should have had for Eric when we went to the mall. *Can you imagine the heads snapping around to get a look at that?*

We still had to go to Costco after our mall disaster. Somewhere between the mall and Costco, my deep worry and panic turned to anger and frustration. While walking through Costco, I imagined sending Eric to the frozen foods area in the back of the building and running out the front door. *How's that for compassion?*

A Blip In Time – Eric Makes A Brief Appearance

NOW I'M GOING TO TELL YOU a story that I have only ever told a few people. In January of 2005, Eric was sitting at the breakfast bar in our living room, reading the paper. He seemed to be having a relatively good day. He looked up from the newspaper and asked me, "Why am I not at work today?"

I'm not sure what it was about the way he asked the question this time because I had answered it many, many times since his surgery. There was something about his tone, something familiar about his inflection. I remember my head snapping up from whatever I was doing to look at Eric. I had goose bumps. *Oh my God, could it be?* It was Eric. My Eric, my "old" Eric, sitting there right in front of me!

I asked him, "Do you remember having headaches?"

He said, "Yes."

Then I launched into the whole story. I explained how he had an MRI and CT scan and it was discovered he had a brain tumor. I asked him if he remembered being in the hospital.

He said, "Vaguely." *That usually meant "No, but I just don't want to admit it."*

I told him he had two brain surgeries and was in the hospital three and a half months.

He looked absolutely stunned. It was as if he were hearing this news for the first time. It was my Eric, the man I married. I would have recognized him anywhere. My heart was racing.

I told him that his surgery was two years earlier and now he was attending a rehab program to try and recover because his short-term memory was almost non-existent. I was talking quickly, almost breathless as if I had to get all the information in before I woke up from what seemed like a dream.

Eric said, "Two years ago?" with incredible shock and disbelief.

I said, "Yes. Eric, you wouldn't believe how it has been. You have no short-term memory and you ask me the same questions over and over because you can't remember that you already asked them. You are obsessed with softball and think you still play like you did when you were twenty and sometimes you get really mean and yell when I tell you that you don't play anymore. It's been really hard but we're doing ok. We are working hard to get you better."

After a few seconds of silence that seemed like several hours, Eric said in a really hushed voice, "I'm sorry about all of this."

My eyes filled with tears. I assured him it was ok and told him we would get through this.

He asked again, "Why am I not at work today?"

I told him he was no longer able to work because of the impact on his memory from the brain surgery.

He got panicked and said, "I've got to get a job." I told him not to worry and he asked almost frantically, "What are we living on?"

"We're getting social security and disability. Don't worry. Just concentrate on getting better."

He was still very confused, but seemed to calm down a little. Then he said the nicest words to me. He said, "I don't know what I'd do without you."

I couldn't hold it in anymore. I started crying. It was too much. Here he was, Eric, sitting right in front of me. I always hoped I'd see him again, but never knew if it would ever happen. Not only was he here, but he was appreciative for all I had done and sorry about how he had behaved.

I hugged Eric and we were silent for about five minutes. When I looked at Eric again, I could tell my old Eric was gone. It was as if the fog had rolled in again.

I asked Eric, "Do you remember what we were just talking about?"

He said, "No."

I could almost hear my heart break. I tried to remind him, but he had no recollection. He looked down at the newspaper that was in front of him and that was the end of it. It was like I had him in my grasp, but he slipped through my fingers.

It was such a gift, those less than 15 minutes I had with *my* Eric. I felt like I lost him all over again and it made me miss him even more.

There was no obvious reason why, all of a sudden, Eric had those lucid minutes. There was no change in his medications or routine that would have triggered a change.

That night, when we went to bed, I felt a closeness to Eric that I hadn't felt in a long time. I was feeling genuine love for him. I knew the post-surgery, confused Eric was back, but I was thrilled that when Eric had those few minutes of clarity, his main concerns were for the kids and me. He was sorry for his bad behavior and grateful for what I had been doing. I looked at the confused Eric and knew he couldn't help how he was. Yes, I felt genuine love. Oh, and by the way, it is like riding a bike.

Later that year, I rented the movie "The Notebook." It was an excellent movie. The supporting characters were played by James Garner and Gena Rowlands. In the movie they were married and she suffered from Alzheimer's.

She had a "clarity" moment in the movie and asked her husband, "How long do we have?" James Garner's character replied, "I don't know, last time it was only about five minutes." It was just like what I experienced with Eric. I only told a few people about that incident because I thought they'd think I was crazy or that it was just "wishful thinking." It definitely happened and I was very grateful for it.

PART
FOUR

Let's Get a Job... or Not Quite
the Promised Land

Oh, Accounting We Will Go

ERIC'S YEAR AT ANIXTER'S government-funded "New Focus" program had come to an end and Eric had no luck with their outplacement program. I wasn't sure what I was going to do. I couldn't have Eric just hanging around the house all day.

Fortunately, his brother had a connection with the local branch of the Hyatt Hotel and Eric's next job was in the accounting department at the Hyatt.

Eric's job coach, Julie, was provided courtesy of the Department of Rehabilitation Services. She was very sweet. Her job was to learn Eric's daily tasks, write instructions, and set up a system so Eric would be able to perform the duties of his job.

Easier said than done. You wouldn't believe how difficult it is to maneuver through life when you have no short-term memory. Eric started the job at the Hyatt in April of 2005 and by September, we all agreed that it wasn't going to work out.

The job consisted of matching up invoices and putting them in certain files at various points of the process. Eric just couldn't keep the system straight. He seemed to catch on early in the job, but then, out of the blue, he would do everything in reverse order. He had notes posted around his work area and a step-by-step to-do list written out for him, but Eric couldn't remember what his ultimate goal was. He would get confused about where he was in the process.

Mondays were especially bad for Eric. It seemed after being away from the job for two days he was extra confused on Mondays.

Just like we trained him with taking the train when he traveled downtown, I trained Eric how to get up to the accounting office from the employee entrance. He had to enter through the employee entrance and travel through the bowels of the hotel. He walked through the laundry area, went up another set of stairs and through a hallway of guestrooms before he arrived at the accounting department.

I, too, trained for the job along with Eric, so I could learn what he would be doing, and even got lost a few times on my way to accounting. Eventually, Eric learned his route and had no problem finding his way.

At the end of each day, I'd park the van, with the kids, outside the employee entrance and wait for Eric. The system worked pretty well with only a few glitches. One time, we were waiting for Eric and it was about fifteen minutes past the time he usually came out. I called up to the accounting department and they told me he left at the regular time. When I told them he never came out of the building, Francis, the man who worked with Eric, said he would grab a few people from the department to find him and bring him out. About twenty minutes later, Eric and a girl from accounting came walking out of the employee entrance. I breathed a sign of relief. I was picturing Eric wandering through uncharted territory of the hotel. The girl told me they found Eric sitting out by the pool. *Go figure, a little lounging time.*

The manager told me later that as he was handing out the paychecks, he joked with Eric about drinks being on him out by the pool, now that he had gotten paid. I can't imagine that Eric would have remembered that, but I guess we'll never know.

One of the perks of the hotel job was that Eric was able to eat lunch for free in the employee cafeteria. One man's perk is another wife's nightmare. Eric already had eating issues and I was a nervous wreck about what he would eat and how much. He ate lunch with his job coach, Julie, everyday and she told me that he only ate two lunches a few times. At one point, he wasn't using tongs to grab the lettuce for salad or other foods. He'd just reach in with his hands. *Oh geez.*

It was "Julie the Job Coach" who called me and told me that Eric wasn't progressing in the job and it was her opinion that he probably wouldn't get to a point where he could ever do the job independently.

I will always be grateful to the general manager of the hotel, at the time, Norm Canfield, for giving Eric the opportunity. I was especially thankful to Francis and the girls who worked with Eric in the accounting department as well as Julie, the job coach. They were patient, kind and treated Eric with respect. As Eric's spouse, I couldn't ask for anything more.

Many months after Eric left the hotel job, a social worker told me that working with numbers was not an ideal job for someone with a traumatic brain injury. Who knew? We took the only opportunity we had and gave it our best shot. Now it was back to the drawing board.

Goodbye Granny

IN SEPTEMBER OF 2005, my mom passed away while she was in town visiting from Las Vegas for several weeks. Her health was on the decline. She was a lifetime smoker, suffered from emphysema, and who-knows-what else. She refused to go to the doctor to find out. It was quite a blessing that she passed away while she was in town with all her kids surrounding her.

Her death was the hardest thing I had to go through in my entire life. My mom and I were best friends and I talked to her on the phone every day. She was a huge source of strength for me and, as I have shared, helped me tremendously when Eric got sick.

We had a beautiful memorial service for my mom. The loss I felt was indescribable. It was so hard to believe she was gone. Eric attended the memorial service for my mom, too, but of course, he couldn't retain anything in his memory.

For several months after my mom passed away, Eric would ask me at least once a day, "Where's your mom?" I'd have to re-explain to Eric that she passed away, and each time, it was like he was hearing the news for the first time. It was painful for me—like pouring salt on a wound and also reminded me that my husband, for all intents and purposes, was gone too.

From Coloring to Dishwashing

IT WAS SEPTEMBER 2005 and I was, once again, without a plan for Eric. It always boggled my mind that I lived in the Chicago metropolitan area and couldn't find any resources for Eric.

Soon, it was late fall and the holidays were approaching - not a good time to look for a job. So, Eric was home with me for the next three months, which was quite a challenge. Let's face it, no one wants to be around their spouse 24 hours a day, 7 days a week when they are perfectly healthy, let alone if they have a brain injury and ask you the same questions all day long.

Downtime was not Eric's friend. It seemed to give his mind time to wander and think up all kinds of crazy things. Then, three o'clock would kick in and he'd start his softball routine.

Needless to say, my nerves were shot. I've often said if you took a picture of me in 2003, when Eric was first diagnosed, and took another one at the end of this whole ordeal, the aging process would be pronounced. It is just like they do with the Presidents, compare photos from when they first took office to photos at the end of their presidency. Let me tell you, gray curls are not attractive. Thank goodness for hair dye.

When the new year arrived, I continued searching for something for Eric to do during the day, but was having no luck. In February of 2006, I went into the senior center that was just two blocks from our home and explained my situation.

They had a four-hour adult daycare program that offered a safe and supportive environment for senior citizens with mild to moderate memory loss. It was also designed to give loved ones a break from their care-giving responsibilities. Eric was no senior citizen, but I needed a break. It must have been obvious because they allowed Eric into the program.

This situation was not ideal. The program offered activities perfect for seniors, such as chair exercises, ring toss, chair dancing, and chair bowling. *Are you seeing a pattern here?* They had sing-a-longs, reminiscing, card games and arts and crafts. Eric was obviously too young for these types of activities, but it served its purpose while I continued searching for something else.

On the plus side, the center was only a few blocks from our home, so I was able to help Eric cross one busy street between our house and the center and watch him walk the rest of the way.

As was the case with the previous programs and jobs I found for Eric, the people were incredibly nice. Heather Schuhrke, the social service representative, was very kind to Eric. I don't know if the people who work at these types of programs really understand the amount of gratitude families feel when their loved one is safe and treated with respect.

Sometimes, I took Alex and Tommy with me on a walk to pick up Eric from the center at the end of the day. Once, we walked in while everyone was coloring. Alex asked, "Why is Daddy coloring?"

I said, "Because it's fun. We like to color, right?"

That was the end of the conversation. Like I said, the program wasn't ideal for Eric, but it served its purpose at the time.

I had been keeping in touch with the department of rehabilitation and our social worker told me that Eric would be able to participate in a work evaluation program run by a branch of the Anixter Center. Participants in this program would work and be trained in an "on the job" type atmosphere and then evaluated by the program personnel.

The goal of the program was to determine whether the participants were capable of learning a job and demonstrating acceptable behaviors. If they passed, the program would assist in placing the pupil in a job.

The program was located inside the employee cafeteria of a Westin Hotel, near the airport, about a twenty-five minute drive from our house.

There was a pay-as-you-go transportation program, and you had to call a day ahead for a ride. Transportation was awarded on a first call, first serve basis. Once the van was full each day, you had to provide your own transportation.

It was probably easier to get Springsteen tickets than schedule a ride for Eric. You could start calling at 5:30 a.m. during the week, so I set my alarm and spent the first 45 minutes of the day hitting the redial button like a Pavlovian dog. When I did get through, a recorded message played over and over until a live person answered.

One thing I knew for sure was that "my call was very important to them and a dispatcher would be with me shortly." *Shortly was a relative term.* A few times, I fell asleep while I waited, and woke to another recording telling me to please hang up and try my call again. *Ug.*

Eric was trained by the manager of the program. When people were done eating, they brought their trays up to the counter, and Eric would scrape whatever food was left on the plates into the garbage and stack all the dishes into racks for the dishwasher. Someone else ran the dishwasher. Eric then had to unload the clean dishes and put them away. He also had to periodically check the tables in the employee dining room to see if any needed to be wiped off.

According to the manager, Eric did well. He said the one thing in Eric's favor was that he had social skills, a difficult thing to teach. Eric didn't say or do anything offensive to the hotel employees during his limited interaction with them and that impressed the manager.

One sick thing crossed my mind that I never had the guts to ask about, probably because I didn't really want to know the answer, was whether Eric ate any of the food that people left on their plates. The thought of it repulsed me, so I figured the "don't ask, don't tell policy" was ok in this situation.

After the four-week assessment period, the manager thought Eric performed well. He agreed that Eric needed constant supervision in whatever job he ended up doing.

Then came several weeks of the program searching for a job for Eric. They informed me I would have the best results if I searched also and contacted family and friends for any possible job leads for Eric. *I had already been down that road.*

The manager of the program called and said UPS was looking for someone to sort boxes for a 4-hour overnight shift from 11 p.m. – 3 a.m. How in the heck was I going to do that with two small kids at home? Was I going to wake them up at 10:30 at night to drive Eric to his job and go back at 3 a.m.? Give me a break.

It soon became apparent to this manager that it was hard to find a job that provided constant supervision. I asked about the job he was doing in the kitchen for training, but they only used that position for training purposes. I soon stopped hearing from the program manager. Eric was home again with me and the kids for more quality time together.

The Church Job

IN AUGUST OF 2006, my friend Sue told me about a volunteer position open at her church, Willow Creek Community Church, and said she thought of Eric right away. I told her I'd love to meet with the person in charge. Not only did Sue set up the meeting, she attended with me.

We met with a girl named Jen who was the head of the church's facilities group. I told her Eric's story and explained our situation. Jen said that it sounded like a good fit. Eric would be part of a work crew that set up tables and chairs in conference rooms all over the church for different meetings and events. He'd have constant supervision, so he wouldn't have to remember what he was supposed to do; someone would always be there to remind him. Best of all, he wouldn't have to find his way around the church by himself; this place was huge—it had its own campus with many buildings.

The office for the facilities group was located in the downstairs of the main building. I dropped Eric off and Jen had someone from her group meet him in the main lobby and bring him to the office. At the end of the day, someone walked Eric back up to the lobby doors and waited with him until I arrived to pick him up.

His hours were 9:00 a.m. – 2:30 p.m., so I sent him with a brown bag lunch inside his backpack each day. He also had a cell phone, just in case he needed to call me or I needed to contact him.

The initial feedback I got from Jen and her group was good. Jen said her people thought Eric was doing fine, although they sometimes had to repeat instructions. *Tell me about it.*

I wanted to hire someone to drive Eric to and from the church, so I put an ad up at the senior center. While I was searching for a permanent driver, the transportation ministry at our own church, Holy Family Parish, arranged volunteer drivers.

Bill S. led the transportation ministry. He was wonderful and the volunteers in the ministry, who drove Eric, couldn't have been more empathetic and respectful. Eventually, I hired a woman to drive

Eric and we were off into our new routine of Eric volunteering at the church.

This was a very stable time for our family. Eric was going to the church during the week to volunteer and since it was a physical job, he came home tired. Although the softball obsession was still a daily battle, I noticed that Eric didn't put up as much of a fight, probably because he was tired when he got home.

For the most part, things were running smoothly with this volunteer position. Only a small handful of times did we have any glitches with Eric getting lost. The lady who drove Eric went to pick him up one day and he never came out of the building. She called me to tell me this, so I called Eric on his cell phone.

He answered the phone and I asked him where he was. He said, "I'm walking in a building."

I asked, "Is it the church you work in everyday?"

"I'm pretty sure it is," he replied.

I told him to stop someone in the halls and tell them he was lost, but Eric said there wasn't anyone around. I then told him to read any signs he saw in the building, so I could get a clue as to his location.

As he wandered Eric said, "I'm walking into the Promised Land."

I said, "What?"

Eric repeated, "I'm walking into the Promised Land."

I said, "No, don't go there; we're not ready for that yet."

Looking back on this, it made me laugh so much. The church had a children's area they called "The Promised Land." That was where Eric got lost that particular day. He eventually found someone who directed him back to the main lobby and then he went outside to catch his ride home.

"Who's Got Dementia?"

AT THE END OF 2005, I went to a conference on dementia, being held at our local community college. I left notes all over the house for Eric with my cell phone number on them and told him I was going to a conference on dementia. Eric said, "Oh, really? Who's got dementia?"

I said, "Uh, that would be you." As usual he just looked confused by my answer.

I was hoping to find some resources and programs for Eric. The issue with Eric was that he fell through the cracks when it came to finding available programs. He was too young, 46 years old, for an adult daycare center because the minimum age was 55, and he was too old for programs for school-aged kids up to the age of 18. There were plenty of programs for the developmentally disabled, but Eric wasn't developmentally disabled. He was too young to sit in the house all day, but with no short-term memory, there weren't a lot of things he was qualified to do.

During one of the breakout sessions in the conference, I raised my hand and gave a brief synopsis of Eric's story. I asked if the presenter was aware of any resources or programs that existed for someone like Eric. The speaker asked several questions about Eric's age and current situation.

I told her I was taking care of Eric along with our two young children. She said she understood the issue I had with Eric's age and said we should talk further at the end of the day.

When the breakout session ended, I gathered up my notebook and papers, stood up, and turned to leave, finding about twelve people waiting in line to talk to me. They all basically said the same thing. Most of them had a parent who was suffering from dementia and they were helping take care of them. Each person said that my story touched them because they knew how hard the day-to-day existence was with someone who suffered from dementia.

They knew about the repetitive questions and the pain of watching a loved one be so confused and vulnerable. It seemed I had struck a chord with these people because Eric was so young and we had young children. They all wanted to tell me how much they could relate to what I was going through and how much they felt for me.

I never did get any good resources from the conference, but the conversations I had with the people who waited to speak to me, made it worth going. And those people have a lot to do with why I ended up writing this book.

"I'm Still Here"

IN EARLY 2006, three years after his surgery, I took Eric back to the hospital for a neuro-psychological exam. During the lunch break, we walked to the cafeteria in the other building. While we were walking down the hall, I saw the little-old-lady volunteer, who had worked the desk in the family surgical waiting room back in 2003, when Eric had his surgeries. I stopped her, pointed to Eric and said, "I remember you. Three years earlier, my husband, Eric, had brain surgery here and you were working in the waiting room that day."

The sweet little lady said, "Can you believe I'm still here? I've been volunteering here for 14 years."

Then Eric said, "Can you believe I'm still here?" He laughed when he said it, meaning to make a joke. It was a flash of his old personality - quick witted, funny and polite. His comment was a pleasant surprise and made me smile.

PART
FIVE

Seeds of Change

The Great Outdoors

IN OCTOBER OF 2007, the kids were back in school, Tommy, in kindergarten, and Alex, in second grade, and the fall sports season had started. Weekdays, Eric was still going to the church to volunteer and in the evening, we usually had to go to one of Alex's soccer practices or games.

Being busy was a good thing for our family. As I said before, the downtime usually worked against us, as far as Eric's behavior was concerned.

Finally, the softball obsession was dying down. Can you believe it? We would go four or five days in a row without Eric ever mentioning softball, and when he did, it was very easy to get him off the subject. I don't know if it was because we were busy with the kids' activities and he had no time to "dial for dollars," the constant tweaking of the medication dosage or just a change in his brain, but he no longer obsessed about it. Whatever it was, I was grateful to be rid of that softball nightmare after three and a half years with that daily obsession. I had thought it would never go away.

Now, a new issue was rearing its ugly head. A few times, when we would be sitting outside at Alex's soccer games or practices, I noticed a terrible odor all of a sudden. It didn't take me long to figure out that Eric had an issue with his bowels. The crazy part was that Eric would just continue to sit in the lawn chair and watch the kids play soccer as if nothing happened. *Believe me, it was crystal clear that something had happened.*

He never once told me he needed a bathroom. When I would confront him and tell him I think he had an accident and we'd better go find a restroom, he just had a dazed look on his face. He had absolutely no sense of urgency and seemed unaware that he had just filled his pants. I remember thinking how happy I was that soccer was an outdoor sport because the odds were better that maybe nobody noticed.

This new issue really freaked me out. I became the "potty police," asking Eric every time before we left the house if he needed to use the bathroom. There were a handful of times when he would say no and sure enough, he would have an issue while we were out. I already went through the whole "potty thing" with our two kids. I certainly didn't want to deal with it with my 47-year-old husband.

I did everything I could to prevent a problem, including feeding Eric early enough so he would be able to use the bathroom before we went anywhere. Unfortunately, in late October and November, I received several calls from the church requesting that I pick Eric up because he had an accident while volunteering.

The people who worked with Eric described the same scenario. He just continued working and the church personnel had to point out to Eric that he had a problem and needed to use the bathroom.

Eric seemed completely unaware of what was happening. How could he not know he had an accident? Couldn't he feel it and wasn't his sense of smell working?

I told Jen, the head of the facilities group at the church, that I certainly didn't expect her or her crew to have to deal with Eric's bowel issues. I would keep him home until I could resolve the issue. It turned out that Eric never made it back to his volunteer position.

What's Going On In That Head? - November 11, 2007

A BIZARRE SEIZURE EPISODE happened in November. About 1:30 in the morning, Eric woke up and walked to the vanity in our bedroom, saying, "I gotta get to the bar, I gotta get to the bar."

I told him he was dreaming, but he told me he wasn't. I got him back into bed and then the real craziness began. He started speaking in a sing-songy tune, repeating exactly what was in his head. He was lying in bed singing, "I'm in the bed. I'm in the bed. Here I am. I'm in the bed."

I said to him, "Eric what's going on?"

He would sing "Eric what's going? What's going on?"

He was repeating everything I said to him, but he was singing it. After about twenty minutes of this, I went down the hall and woke up his mom.

Eric started down memory lane in his brain. His family used to travel to Harbor Springs, Michigan when Eric was young. Eric started to sing, "There's Mary and Kathleen and Barbara and my brother Tom," all in the same tune. He said they were in Harbor Springs and started to recall his childhood and this trip they would take.

He sang everything in that sing-songy, non-stop tune. Eric started counting down from forty-eight, singing all the way down to: 5, 4, 3, 2, 1, and 0.

Then he repeated, "Re-birth, re-birth, re-birth." He must have repeated the word re-birth about twenty times. That made the hair on my arms stand straight up. Re-birth? What in the world was going on in that head of his? Eric turned forty-eight two weeks prior, is that why he started the count down at forty-eight?

Eric's mom and I kept trying to get him to stay in bed, close his mouth, and go to sleep. No matter what he said, it was in that sing-songy voice. Then Grandma and I decided to take shifts. She told me to go down the hall into her bed to sleep and she would sit up with

Eric, since I had to get up with the kids in the morning. As I lay in her bed, I could hear him singing and talking, so I wasn't getting any sleep.

About twenty minutes later, Grandma came walking into the room and we were both lying in the bed now, listening to Eric singing at the end of the hall. After about twenty more minutes, we went back into his room. He was still lying there, saying anything that was in his mind, all kinds of nonsense, in that sing-songy tone.

Our nightmare was going on two hours old. It was almost 3:30 a.m. and Eric was still going strong with no signs of stopping.

I got an over-the-counter sleeping pill out of our cabinet and brought it to Eric with a glass of water. Without any questions Eric took the pill, drank the glass of water, and stopped singing. He went silent. I looked at Maggie with my finger over my mouth, gesturing shhhhhh. I didn't want her to say anything that he was going to be able to repeat.

I took Eric by the elbow, led him to our bed, laid him down, and covered him up. I went and lay down on my side of the bed and Maggie waited about five minutes, then left our bedroom and that was the end of our nightmare. It was 3:45 a.m.

When Eric woke up in the morning he had absolutely no memory of any part of that incident.

Seizure Disorder

THAT SAME NOVEMBER, I noticed that Eric started displaying some very peculiar behavior. OK, more peculiar behavior than what we were used to. He would stare off into space and I could almost see that he had checked out for the moment. His eyes were glazed over and he could hear me, but wasn't responding when I spoke to him. He would sit at the bar and repeat the same words over and over, like he was stuck.

One day, I looked over at Eric and he just kept saying, "The way it was. The way it was. The way it was," over and over again.

I asked him, "Eric, is something wrong?" He just kept saying, "The way it was. The way it was."

Then I asked him questions that I knew he knew the answers to. "What are the kids' names?"

He said, "The way it was."

"What is my name?"

"The way it was."

He just could not stop repeating that phrase. I pulled the ketchup and mustard out of the refrigerator and said, "Eric what is this?"

He still responded, "The way it was, the way it was."

I showed him the mustard and asked him what it was.

"The way it was, the way it was."

So I put them away.

Within ten minutes or so, I noticed that he had snapped out of the haze he was in. I grabbed the ketchup out of the fridge and asked, "Eric do you know what this is?"

He said, "Ketchup. Why?" As if it was such a ridiculous question.

I said, "How about this?" as I showed him the mustard.

He said, "Mustard. You don't know that's mustard?" he asked me.

"I know what it is, but ten minutes ago you didn't." I told him he just had a weird kind of "episode." Of course, he had no memory of it.

Sometimes, instead of repeating a phrase, Eric would have a repetitive hand motion or an ever-so-slight movement of his fingers.

This was another way these seizures would manifest themselves. He would move his left hand within a three-inch radius, back and forth, back and forth, over and over. I would put my hand on his hand to stop the motion, but I couldn't. It was strong, as if his body *had* to do the movement.

After about ten to fifteen minutes of this repetitive behavior, whether it was repeating a phrase or a body movement, it would end and I could almost see his eyes get clear. After every "episode," he would get extremely tired.

With this bizarre behavior, I jumped to the conclusion that the brain tumor was growing. I made an appointment with the neurosurgeon, he had an MRI, and no, it was not growing. Everything looked the same as it had over the last five years.

They told me at the neurosurgeon's office that what I was describing sounded like partial-complex seizures. I knew what a seizure was, but not a partial-complex seizure. They explained that it was very much like what I had described: the staring off, the glazed look, repetitive words, repetitive motions, that kind of thing.

The episodes were occurring about six or seven times a day. The first appointment with the neurologist for the seizures was on a Monday, November 19, 2007. He prescribed an anti-seizure medication. Every two weeks, Eric would get an adjustment to the dosage by increasing it a little bit, until we saw a decrease in the number of seizures each day, adding, of course, to all of his other medications he was already taking.

We went out to dinner with Eric's parents and the kids the night after he started on the anti-seizure medication. (It was the Tuesday before Thanksgiving.) We had a beautiful dinner. The kids were well behaved, very enjoyable. At the end of dinner, the kids were waiting for their ice cream sundaes and Eric was playing tic-tac-toe on the placemat with Tommy.

Everything was going fine, and then I noticed that Eric's hand was going back and forth in about a three or four inch line with the blue crayon, back and forth, back and forth. Then the motion got a little bigger and a little bigger again. I noticed he had ripped a hole in the placemat.

The motion got bigger, and bigger, and bigger. He started to kind of spit and I knew we had a problem. I asked the hostess to please call 911.

The seizure got progressively worse. The arm movement got bigger. He started making guttural noises that were very loud, and then the paramedics showed up.

There were three or four paramedics and it took all of them to get Eric into the ambulance. I went in the ambulance with Eric. Grandma and Grandpa took the van and went home with the kids.

Eric's seizure increased in intensity during the ambulance ride to the hospital. He started shouting profanity, screaming the F-bomb repeatedly. I kept telling the paramedics, "He never talks this way. He's really a nice guy. I don't know what's happening to him." They assured me they understood, saying that this was just the seizure and he was not in his right mind.

Eric spent three days in the hospital with no other seizure activity and was released to go home the weekend after Thanksgiving.

We continued to go to the neurologist appointments where his anti-seizure medication dosage was adjusted, but the partial-complex seizures continued through December and into January.

Sometimes, Eric would mouth words silently—no noises would come out. He would trace things in mid-air or repeat arm motions for thirty to forty minutes.

One day, we were hanging our Christmas wreaths outside and I realized Eric could not speak. I asked him a question and he looked at me but could not form a word. As I got more familiar with these seizures, I could recognize when he was having one and would ask him, "Eric are you trying to talk, but you just can't get words out?" And he would nod his head, "Yes."

Another way these partial-complex seizures would manifest themselves was when Eric was sitting in his chair, maybe watching TV. All of a sudden, he would take his pointer finger and start tracing a square in mid-air. I would ask him, "Eric, what are you doing."

He would respond, "I am tracing these boxes." He would do that for about fifteen or twenty minutes, then he'd put his hand down and fall asleep.

A few times, I would look over and Eric would be sticking his tongue straight out of his mouth and he would be staring down at the tip of his tongue. I would ask him what he was doing and he'd say, "Sticking my tongue out."

I asked him, "Why?"

He responded, "I don't know. I'm just doing it."

That would last about thirty minutes and then he'd fall asleep.

We had one day that I called, "The day of scratching." Eric would be sitting in his chair and he'd scratch the arm of his chair. Then he'd lean over and scratch the lamp that was next to his chair. He got up and went across the room and started scratching the wall.

Another day, I came into the room with the kids and Eric was bent over against the wall in the family room. I asked him, "Eric, what are you doing?"

He said, "Building a house."

I said, "Building a house? What do you mean?"

He responded, "You know, building and painting." And he was rubbing the wall of the family room.

December came and went, filled with bizarre behavior. January was no different. We were still going to the neurologist appointments, increasing Eric's anti-seizure dosage, but the partial-complex seizures continued. Eric was doing a lot of mumbling to himself, saying the alphabet over and over, counting, finger tracing in the air, and all kinds of nonsense. There seemed to be no end.

One time, I noticed Eric's mouth was moving while he was sitting in his chair and I said, "Hey Eric what are you saying over there?"

He said, "I'm counting."

I asked him "You're counting?"

He said, "Yes."

"Well, what number are you on," I asked him.

And he said, "Two hundred and thirty-two."

I told Eric, "You don't need to count. You know, you could count all the way up to a million if you wanted."

Eric said "Oh don't say that!"

"Why not?" I asked him.

And he said, "Because then I am going to have to count to a million."

I said "No you're not, honey. You know you can. Just try to wipe those numbers out of your mind. You don't need to count, that's not something you have to do."

He just listened, but later I saw his mouth moving again. I was sure he was counting again, hopefully, not to a million.

Another day in early January, Eric was going to bed, but he dropped down onto the floor and did a somersault. Now I don't know about you, but I am in my mid-forties and I can't remember the last time I did a somersault. What in the world came over him? I asked, "Eric, why did you just do a somersault?"

He said, "Because I felt like it."

I said, "Ok. It was a really good one too."

Eric had two incidents within two days that were really very, very odd, even odder than the finger tracing, mumbling, and counting. Eric would start to laugh hysterically. He could not control it and could not stop. It was a deep, loud, bellyache of a laugh, like somebody had told him the funniest joke he had ever heard in his entire life.

As he was laughing hysterically, I asked him "Eric what's so funny? Let me in on the joke; I could use a laugh."

He would try to stop laughing and get a few words out, but then he'd just start all over again, laughing hysterically.

One morning Eric's cousin, Mary, was over and this whole laughing thing started again. She couldn't believe her eyes. We asked him, "Eric what's so funny? We want to get in on the joke."

Just when he would start to calm down and talk, he would lose it again and start laughing. Finally he caught his breath and said, "You guys have it all wrong!"

Mary and I looked at each other confused. I asked Eric "What do we have all wrong?"

And he said, "The rules to the game. You have them all wrong."
He started laughing hysterically again, opened his mouth, head back,
hand on the belly, hysterically laughing. He was drooling out of the
side of his mouth because his mouth was open for so long. This lasted
for close to an hour and was very creepy. When he stopped laughing,
he fell asleep on the couch.

The Bite and The Bizarre

FOR ALMOST FIVE YEARS we were riding this "post-tumor" roller coaster and found ourselves not knowing what our next step was. There were no local resources for someone in Eric's position, he was unable to hold down a job and now he was suffering seizures. He was too young to sit at home and rot for the rest of his life.

Eric's brother had a connection with his wife's cousin who founded an organization called "The Five Fingers Foundation" in Phoenix, Arizona. The foundation cares for and provides services for people who are disabled and in need.

The head of the foundation, Luis, was willing to have Eric reside in Arizona for care. He asked us for a commitment of six months in order to be most effective with Eric's care and rehabilitation.

Luis flew to Chicago to meet the family and finalize the details of Eric's care. We were very close to implementing this plan, but in January, the most disturbing part of Eric's illness occurred. On Friday, January 11th, I got the kids off to school. Within an hour, I got a call from the school nurse asking me to pick up Alex. She had a cold sore on her mouth that the nurse thought might be contagious. I brought her home and called the pediatrician to make an appointment for that afternoon.

Alex was out in the family room, watching cartoons and Eric was sitting at the bar using his magnifying glass to read the paper, as he had everyday for the last five years. I was standing in the kitchen and noticed Eric's magnifying glass lying right next to the paper. I asked him, "Eric. Don't you want to use your magnifying glass to read the newspaper?"

He looked at me and said "Yes." Then he stood up from the barstool.

I told him, "The magnifying glass is right there next to you."

"Yeah, ok," he replied, and kept staring at me as he got off the barstool and walked around the side of the bar and into the kitchen where I was standing. I told him again that he didn't need to get out of his chair, that the magnifying glass was right there and he just said, "Ok."

He kept walking toward me and I noticed that he had a very glassy look in his eyes. I asked Eric what he was doing.

He said, "I am coming in here by you."

I said, "Oh." And with that, he reached his hands out and grabbed my forearms. He lowered his head and led with his shoulder, putting his body weight against mine in a constant pressure maneuver, causing me to start walking backward in order to stay vertical.

"Eric what are you doing? You are pushing me and squeezing my arms really hard and it hurts. Why are you pushing me?" I asked as we walked backward.

He said, "I am feeling a little pushy." I knew Alex was in the family room, so I turned and walked backward down the main hall toward our office. I continued to walk backward and dropped down on the love seat in our office. Eric leaned forward with all his weight and leaned against me, practically crushing me.

I said, "Eric you are still pushing against me and squeezing my forearms. Please let go! What's going on?"

Then I saw Alex, our daughter, standing in the door of the office with the cordless telephone. She asked me very nervously, "What's going on?"

I told her, "I don't know. I think Daddy might be having a seizure. Why don't you hand me the phone." I dialed the phone with just my one hand and asked my friend Katina from down the street to come over. I was trying to remain very calm because Alex looked nervous and I didn't want to scare her.

Eric was leaning against my body with all of his weight and his head was upside down and he still had a grip on my forearms and he was squeezing very, very tightly. I don't think he realized it. I think he was having a seizure.

I kept telling him, "Eric, you need to sit on your butt. Your head is upside down and you do not need more pressure on your head. You need to get your weight off me, you are crushing me, and it hurts. Eric please, sit down. Sit on your butt and get your head upright."

Finally, after what seemed like forever, Eric did right his body and sat down, continuing to hold my forearms in a death grip with my left arm draped across his chest. He opened his mouth and took a big chomp down into my arm right at the bend of the elbow. Excruciating pain shot right through me and I couldn't help but scream at the top of my lungs.

Unfortunately, our daughter Alex was standing right there. She saw it happen and started screaming and hollering. I told her, "Honey it's ok. It's ok. Daddy doesn't know what he is doing. He is not in his right mind."

But after he took that bite, he did not take his mouth off my arm. I was yelling at Eric and telling him, "Eric please, you have got to open your mouth. You just bit me in the arm and it really hurts. You've got to let go of my forearms. Please Eric, please, you are hurting me."

Alex ran outside, waiting for my friend to show up and was screaming and crying in terror. When Katina walked in the front door, I told her to call 911. "Eric just bit me and I think he is having a seizure," I said.

I heard my girlfriend calling 911, explaining the situation, while I continued to talk to Eric. "Eric, please take your mouth off my arm. You're hurting me. Please let go of my arm. It hurts. I am bleeding. You bit me. Let go of my arm, please!"

No response at all. He just stared with glassy eyes. Finally, after what seemed like forever, Eric took his mouth off my arm and let go of my forearms. He then got off the love seat, dropped to his knees in our office, and did a somersault. He popped up, jogged in place a little bit, and then walked out into our entryway. Our front door was open from when Katina came into the house and Eric draped both arms over the top of our front door, one on each side and dug his fingernails into the top part of our wood door.

The paramedics showed up. Two guys came in and they had to call for backup because Eric was so strong and he was fighting them. They had to rip his nails out of the wooden door and get him seated and calmed down so that they could check him out. Eric was uncooperative and bent his knees as if he was performing some kind of wrestling maneuver. He was trying to take down the paramedics. Soon more paramedics showed up.

As it had in the restaurant in November, the seizure seemed to escalate in intensity. He started with the spitting again. He started shouting profanity. Repetitive profanity. Thank goodness, at this point, Katina had taken Alex outside and they were on their way to her house.

Eric was getting more and more out of control. They gave him an intramuscular shot to calm him down and it didn't seem to have any affect on him at all. I know they gave him another one before they loaded him into the ambulance.

One of the paramedics had taken me back into the office to get all the details and the history on Eric's behavior.

Eric was a mess. He had drool all over his face, he was panting and swearing. *Who was this man and where was my husband?*

Again I was explaining, "He never swears like this. This is so unlike his personality."

The paramedics assured me they understood and told me to go to the emergency room and have my arm checked. They explained that a human bite was one of the dirtiest you could get because of all the germs people had in their mouths. They said I could see Eric in the hospital after I was taken care of.

When the paramedics left, I closed the door and stood there, all alone in the house. What in the world just happened here? What made Eric approach me and do this? In the five years since his brain surgery, he had never, EVER, demonstrated any aggressive physical behavior. What in the world was going through his mind? I had to believe that he was unable to control himself.

I knew that biting was fairly common during seizures, but I had never ever been afraid of Eric before that day. I was so scared now, and the more I thought of the possible things that could have happened, I started to tremble and cry. I wondered, *Where was all this going to end? What if that had been Alex instead of me? Why did she have to be home the one day that this terrible incident happened?* I thought, *She would have been in school normally and missed the whole episode. That sweet girl had enough trouble dealing with all of the issues surrounding her dad. The last thing she needed was to witness this.*

I went to the emergency room and got my arm looked at. They cleaned me up and then I went to visit Eric in the emergency room. Eric, of course, had absolutely no memory of biting me, or any part of the incident at all.

What followed next was a nightmarish six days of hospitalization. Eric was not a cooperative patient and caused all kinds of trouble for the staff.

I made sure to explain to the staff about his short-term memory loss, but like other times, until they saw it, nobody really seemed to believe me.

The neurologist continued to adjust Eric's anti-seizure medication during the six days in the hospital. One day, I got a call reporting that Eric got out of his bed and crawled under the other bed in the room. What in the world was that all about? I had no idea. The behavior just got more and more bizarre.

They also wouldn't let Eric out of his bed during this hospital stay, which drove him absolutely crazy. At one point, they had to restrain him. If someone tried to keep me in bed for six days straight, they would need to restrain me too.

The doctors were ready to discharge Eric, but because he had not been out of bed in six days they wanted to discharge him to a rehab facility for physical therapy and speech therapy to help him get back on his feet.

As for me, I was scared to have Eric come home. What if he hurt someone again? I had to protect the kids and I didn't know what to do.

Giving me a little reprieve, one week after Eric bit me, he got transferred to a rehab facility for physical, occupational, and speech therapy. Eric's mom and I packed up some sweat pants and T-shirts, brought them to the rehab facility, and got him settled in.

The next day, I went to visit Eric with my brother, Butch, and the kids. This rehab facility was also a nursing home. When we walked into the door, we had to travel two very long hallways before getting to Eric's room.

We had one foot in the door and one of our kids said, "This place smells like poop," and the other one chimed in, "and like pee."

I turned around, looked at them and said, "I know it does, but please do not yell that out loud. Just follow me. We are going to Daddy's room."

The two long hallways seemed never-ending and they were crowded with very elderly people sitting in wheelchairs. They had hopeless looks in their eyes.

I remember seeing one lady, everyday, when I would visit Eric. She would sit in the doorway to her room, facing the hallway and say, "Would someone please help me. Would someone please help me," over and over again.

The staff in the hallway would just pass by her, going about their day, doing their work. No one paid attention to this poor soul.

Finally, one day I asked her, "What can I help you with Ma'am?"

She said she needed to get the water out of her cupboard. Well, of course she didn't have a cupboard, she was in a nursing home, but I asked if she would like a glass of water and she said, "Yes."

I asked a nurse if I could give this woman a glass of water and she said, "Sure."

I handed her a glass of water and the woman said, "Well what about the water in my cupboard?"

I told her, "Well, when I come back here tomorrow, if you still need help with the water in your cupboard, I will come and help you."

Her eyes met mine and she said, "Thank you very much!"

I couldn't help but think, maybe she was just waiting for someone to acknowledge her. Once I was gone, she probably started back up with the "will someone please help me" routine. It's heartbreaking to see people like that.

As we reached the end of the hall, we finally arrived at Eric's room. We walked in and I couldn't believe what I saw. Eric was sitting in a wheelchair, his chin to his chest, head down in a complete stupor.

I walked in and said, "Hi honey it's us! It's Butch, Alex, and Tommy." No response. I said, "Eric, How are you?" I could tell something was very wrong. I went down to the nurses' station, told them I was Eric's wife and spoke with his nurse. They said they would send somebody down to his room, so I went back and tried to chit-chat with Eric.

Once the nurse arrived in Eric's room, the first question she asked was, "Can Eric speak?"

I just about had a heart attack. I said, "Of course Eric can speak! What is going on? Why is he like this? Yes, he can speak."

She said, "Oh. Well, he hasn't said much."

I kept asking questions. "What is wrong with him? Did something happen to him? Has he been getting his medications?"

Then the nurse gasped, as if to say, "Huh! Medications?"

I asked, "He hasn't been getting his medications?"

She went on to explain that it was her understanding that they were waiting for pharmacy to deliver Eric's medications.

I told her "No. His medications were brought here yesterday when he arrived." She went to the front desk to look into the mix up.

Eric was a step away from a drool cup. Here were the kids coming to visit him for the first time and he was in a complete stupor. I had to throw a fit at the rehab facility.

We sat and visited with Eric and I was aggravated the entire time. I could not get past the fact that this facility had not given Eric any of his medications. He looked terrible.

The kids seemed uncomfortable. I am sure they didn't like seeing their dad in that condition. I know I didn't like seeing my husband in such a state.

Next Up: Bill-The-Roommate

ERIC WAS IN A ROOM WITH A MAN named Bill. Bill was shaking his head when all this happened and when all the nurses left the room, he gave us his two cents on the facility and the lack of supervision. "Eric was wandering around the halls last night. I found him and brought him back to our room."

He said that whenever he notices Eric out of the room, he takes a little wheelchair ride down the hall to find out where he is, just to make sure he's not wandering. "Last night, Eric wandered around for about an hour before I found him," Bill added. *What are these people thinking?*

I visited Eric everyday and sat in on three of his therapy sessions for physical, speech, and occupational therapy. Although the first day was lousy, he seemed to be getting better everyday. The physical therapist told me how impressed he was and how much progress he thought Eric was making, as did the speech and occupational therapists.

As he improved, I'd shoot the breeze with Eric, bring him to one of the activity sessions and then head back home to see the kids after school.

On Thursday morning of the week that Eric was in rehab, my phone rang at 5:30. *As I said before, it's never good when the phone rings too early.*

It was the rehab center. They said that Eric's roommate woke up to Eric strangling him. *Bill the roommate, who did nothing but help Eric since he arrived, woke up to Eric strangling him.*

How could this possibly be? They informed me that they took Eric to the hospital and I could come and clean out all of his things.

Eric's mom and I went to the rehab facility to gather Eric's belongings. I wanted to speak with Bill, his roommate, but he was at the emergency room getting checked over.

While we were there, some of the people at the desk were giving us details about what they heard happened.

When Eric strangled Bill, Bill hit the call button and several staff members went into the room. As they told it, with every staff member who went into the room, Eric "went after them."

They called the paramedics and Eric supposedly "went after" the paramedics as well. They had to call the police. They told us that the police tasered Eric once and it did nothing. They said the police tasered Eric a second time, pepper sprayed him, and handcuffed him.

When they told me this story, I felt like my stomach dropped to my toes. Dear Lord. How could this possibly happen to Eric? The gentlest man I had ever met. What happened to him? What would go through his mind that he would try to strangle his roommate, who had been so kind to him?

The only thing I could think of is that he was having some terrible, terrible thoughts running through his mind. They said that he looked as if he were cornered and threatened and that was why he fought the paramedics and police.

This time, they put Eric in the critical care unit of the hospital. This, the day after Eric strangled his roommate, Eric had one of his most lucid days in five years. His brother and sister-in-law, his dad, and I, all visited him in the critical care unit. He was calm, cordial, and talking very politely.

He looked like he had gone ten rounds with Muhammad Ali in his prime. He had a very, very large bump on the corner of his forehead. I imagined that was from when he fell after getting tasered for the second time. He looked terrible, but mentally he was very lucid and polite, better than I had seen him in a very long time.

Eric only spent a day on the critical care floor and then was transferred to the sixth floor of the hospital. After a couple days, he was transferred to the eighth floor. *Movin' on up.*

Hallucinations... or "Breaking the Pen"

HE WAS NOT A GOOD PATIENT. Something was happening to Eric's mind. He started to get crazy, literally deranged, insane. The next four days in the hospital were the worst ever, in five years. Eric was paranoid and he was hallucinating.

One day, I was sitting there and he started to look up at the ceiling, his eyes darting back and forth as if he were following a mosquito. I watched him and his gaze came down the wall just over my shoulder and he whispered, "Wendy! Look at all those headless men. Do you see them? Do you see them all?"

And I said, "Eric, honey. There are no headless men."

He said, "Yes there are. They're right there above your shoulder; can't you see them all? *What in God's name is happening to my husband?*"

This was the start of Eric getting no sleep for thirty hours straight. He would not go to sleep. He would not close his eyes. He was paranoid. He was telling me during a phone conversation that he thought the police were coming for him and he told me he had to break the pen.

I asked him, "Break the pen? What are you talking about Eric? Are you writing? Are you holding a pen?"

He said, "No. I've got to break the pen."

I said, "Eric, I don't know what you are talking about. What do you mean you've got to break the pen?"

He said, "The penitentiary. I am going to break out of the penitentiary."

The best I could put together is that he thought the metal bars on the side of his hospital bed were jail bars and he was going to break out.

The nurse called me one night and said that I had to get over to the hospital because Eric was trying to break his bed and they had to call hospital security two times that night.

I asked the nurse to put him on the phone and I talked to him from home for about forty-five minutes. He told me the police were coming for him and I said "No Eric, that's hospital security and as long as you calm down they will go away. They just want you to calm down. You think they are police officers and I can understand that honey, they have the same looking uniforms, but it's not the police. They are hospital security and you just need to calm down and everything will be ok."

It was the saddest thing in the world, having to talk to my husband this way. I couldn't believe he really didn't have one foot in reality whatsoever.

When he didn't think the police were after him, he thought he had all kinds of work meetings. He would do lap, after lap, after lap around the nurses' station, poking his head into all the rooms on the floor, looking for the person he had a meeting with.

Eric was crazy, absolutely out of his mind. It was a constant struggle to talk some sense into him. We finally realized that the best thing was to just go along with whatever he was thinking and try to divert his attention. My sister-in-law, Patti, was so great with Eric during this hospital stay. She went along with Eric and participated in many 'important' meetings (wink, wink) with him and long 'business discussions'. She was awesome.

The staff was clearly afraid of Eric because he was so big and so agitated. When the hospital personnel would come into the room to tend to Eric's roommate, they would practically walk with their backs against the wall, so that they wouldn't have to turn their back on Eric.

They were calling me at all hours of the night and telling me that I had to get to the hospital because Eric was so out of control. They finally had to restrain him, which was not a pleasant sight.

What in the world happened to Eric? Why was this happening?

As is my experience with hospitals, it's almost impossible to get more than one doctor in front of you at the same time. I had to pull a "Shirley McClain" and throw an absolute fit, demanding to see not only the psychiatrist, but also the hospital physician and the neurologist.

I lined them up in the hallway and I said, "Listen. This is ridiculous. What is happening to this man? He has lost his mind. He is literally insane and we don't know why. He is paranoid and he is hallucinating. What is happening to Eric?"

All three doctors just stared right back at me and nobody spoke up. When I pushed for answers, one of the doctors offered the following explanation: Although an MRI didn't show any shift in Eric's brain, his brain might have shifted a little. They said that the combination of all the medications Eric had been taking over the past five years, along with Eric's own physiology, was causing this reaction.

I asked, "What treatment is available and what are my options?"

None of the doctors had any suggestions. The psychiatrist said that the only scenario he saw was an institutional setting for Eric, but that it would not be ideal because Eric was very different from others in that setting.

This whole situation was crazy. I said, "We are giving Eric medications and they are poisoning him, making him, literally, insane. We have to stop giving him his medication."

The hospital physician said, "Well, that will kill him."

I raised my voice and angrily replied, "Look at him right now. That is no longer our worst case scenario."

Reaching Out to Hospice

IT WAS NOT EASY WATCHING ERIC lose his mind in front of my very eyes. The poor, gentle, loving man was ripping the hospital apart, hallucinating, and paranoid that people were out to get him. Eric would not have wanted to live this way. That was something we all agreed on.

The hospital physician said I would have to meet with Hospice if we were thinking of taking Eric off his medications.

"Then get me a meeting with Hospice because I need to help this man."

After a family meeting, we decided to stop Eric's medications. My main concern was that I wanted him to receive Hospice care, which is comfort care as somebody leaves this life. He was a very unique case, uncharted territory. That's what we had been hearing for the last five years.

After several meetings with various levels in the Hospice organization and the hospital, Friday, February 1st was Eric's first day without any medications. He slept for most of the day, not surprising after thirty very hyper hours with no sleep. He had expended a huge amount of energy in those thirty hours.

The doctors told us that without his medications, Eric's death would happen quickly, three or four days, maximum, and he would be gone. It goes without saying that this was not an easy decision. And so, the waiting began.

The next two days Eric was sleepy, but had quite an appetite. He was responsive and walked many laps around the nurses' station. He would rest and sleep, then walk, and rest and sleep, and walk again. Eric was back to his old self, laughing and joking with everyone. He was more lucid than he had been in a long time. Eric actually knew who was running for president.

The Hospice people were quick to tell us that when people were on their way out of this world, it was very common that they have a surge of energy. It was even written in the Hospice pamphlet they gave us. It said that people who were once disoriented, became clear minded. People who had no appetite, became hungry. People who were not social at all, were chatting with people they hadn't talked to in a long time.

They saw us get our hopes up when Eric started acting so normally again after four straight days of insanity. Hospice told us that this behavior was part of the death process, and to look at this quality time we had with Eric as a gift. Four days came and went. Eric was sleepy some days, but strong. The Hospice people were amazed at how well Eric was doing. Things were certainly not going as predicted.

This is our last family picture taken in the hospital, two weeks before Eric died.

Hospice informed us that they had to discharge him from the hospital and asked us if he'd be coming home. I knew I couldn't bring Eric home for two reasons: Number one, I didn't want the kids to have to watch their dad die in their own home, and two, I didn't know if he was done with his aggressive behavior. I had to protect the kids. They had to come first.

This sparked heated debate within the family regarding where Eric was going to go. Eric's mom and I visited several nursing homes and I knew I could never send Eric to any of those places with a clear conscience. For me, it was out of the question.

It was decided that Eric would go to Miami with his brother and sister-in-law and stay with them, then when appropriate his brother would travel with Eric to Phoenix and get him settled at the Five Fingers Foundation with Patti's cousin. Hospice would discharge him from Illinois and pick him back up in Florida.

The hospital physician taking care of Eric told me he thought the prognosis was the same, just that they must have had the timing wrong. His theory was that Eric was still going strong because he was a big guy and his system may have been taking longer to clear out the medications.

The doctor was dead set against Eric getting on an airplane. He said to us, "What if he gets violent? How are you going to handle him if he gets violent? The pilot will take that plane down if he has to."

Our plan was that we would give Eric an anti-anxiety pill at the airport before they got on the plane and hopefully he would sleep most of the way. The weather was bad and the flight was delayed an hour-and-a-half, so they ended up giving Eric two badly needed anti-anxiety pills.

Tom and Patti told me Eric kept looking all over O'Hare airport for me. "Where's Wendy?" he would say. "Where's Wendy? Wendy was just here. Wendy's got to get on the plane with us."

They said that he almost didn't get on the airplane because I wasn't there. They had to lie to him and say, "Wendy's in Miami and if you don't get on the plane and we arrive in Miami without you, Wendy will be very upset."

He finally did get on the plane and, for the most part, he was fine. He slept a majority of the flight. However, when the plane landed, he could barely walk. His left leg was not working at all. His brother had to support almost all his weight and walk him down the jet way until they arrived at the prearranged wheelchair.

The first few days in Miami were very bad. Eric was confused. He got up and wandered. His blood pressure was very, very low. Eric's parents arrived two days later and helped take care of him. The new Hospice had arrived with a nurse and an attendant to shower and shave Eric and get the details of his case.

The next few days, Eric played cards, read, and slept a lot. He had a good appetite and was very talkative. His walk was a little unbalanced sometimes, but for the most part, ok.

One day, they even took Eric to a driving range. I had to laugh when I heard this on the phone. We all said, "Let's hope that Hospice doesn't show up today to check on Eric. Can you imagine? 'Hey, where's Eric?' 'Oh! He's at the driving range, hitting some balls.'"

The driving range didn't go so well. Eric got dizzy at one point and stumbled forward several yards. They sat him on a bench until he felt better and later he practiced putting on the putting green. The rest of the day, Eric slept. The driving range experience had wiped him out.

Later on that week, Eric was doing well. A second Hospice doctor called looking for information about the medications Eric had been taking before. By then, he was only taking the anti-seizure medications.

We had a very long conversation with this Hospice doctor, who seemed to take a real interest in Eric's case. The doctor seemed to think that Eric's pituitary was functioning, at least partially. Otherwise, he wouldn't be alive.

The doctor proposed we take Eric off the remaining medications, including a medication that stopped his repetitive thoughts. We all agreed. The doctor said, "If we're going to live, it's without medications."

Hey, I was all for that. I was tired of going to the pharmacy and picking up and administering pills, shots, and nasal sprays to Eric. And now that the medications seemed to be poisoning Eric, I wanted them gone. I'm sure Eric was sick of it too.

The doctor said that we had to assume that Eric was in a terminal condition, and although he didn't want to get our hopes up, there was a very slight, slight chance that it wasn't terminal.

The only reaction Eric's body had to getting off all the medications was the first day he urinated "a ton" while he was still in the hospital. That lasted about a day, as it had the previous time. Then his urination re-regulated itself, almost like a computer that reboots itself. As long as he kept eating and drinking, there was no fear of dehydration. And Eric's eating and drinking were fine.

When he was feeling a bit better, everyday, about four o'clock in the afternoon, Eric would start obsessing at Tom and Patti's house looking for his keys. He'd say, "I'm looking for my keys. Where are my keys?"

They would explain to him that his keys were at home in Chicago and that he was in Miami on vacation.

Eric would respond by saying, "Ok. Well, then can I use your keys? Because I am going to go out to the clubs."

They told him, "No, you can't have our keys and you can't drive our cars because you aren't covered under our insurance."

Eric then asked, "Ok, well, then where are your yellow pages? I am going to call a cab because I am going out to the clubs."

This happened every late afternoon for the last five or six nights of his stay. This made me laugh so much because it reminded me of the softball routine I had dealt with for so many years. I teased Tom, saying that since arriving in Miami, Eric quit softball and had become a clubber.

Who's Up for South Beach? — March 1ˢᵗ, 2008

ERIC WAS DOING WELL and we decided to go ahead with the rehab program in Phoenix, Arizona. Grandma and Grandpa had changed their plane tickets and were going back home to Hilton Head on Tuesday, March 4ᵗʰ. Tom and Patti decided that since it was Saturday and a gorgeous day in Miami, they would all go out for a nice lunch.

They went to South Beach, about a forty-five minute drive, and had lunch about three o'clock in the afternoon and then took a walk several blocks down Lincoln Road, where there are lots of shops and sidewalk cafés.

About six o'clock in the evening, they went into another restaurant and had dessert. South Beach is a popular nightspot and it was beginning to get crowded.

Everyone was enjoying their dessert, when Eric stood up and said he had to use the bathroom. The bathrooms were upstairs in this restaurant and Grandma told brother Tom to please go upstairs with Eric.

When they got in the men's room, all the urinals were taken. Tom directed Eric into a stall and told Eric he would go in the one next to him and they would meet outside the stalls in a couple minutes.

When Tom came out of the stall, Eric was nowhere to be found. He said it was as if he vanished. He yelled his name, "Eric! Eric!" and searched the entire bathroom looking for Eric, but he was gone.

Since Eric did not move very quickly, Tom just figured that when he walked out the door, Eric would be half-way down the steps. But, there was no sign of Eric anywhere. Tom went downstairs, found the rest of the group, and said, "Eric is gone."

Patti, my sister-in-law, explained to me that there was a police officer on every block of Lincoln Road. She said that within one minute of Tom coming down and telling them Eric was gone, they were talking to one of the police officers outside. That officer then got on his walkie-talkie and alerted the rest of the police monitoring

Lincoln Road of the fact that Eric was missing. He also explained his mental disability and that he had no memory or self-awareness.

Tom and Patti filed a police report and since Eric was very much like an Alzheimer's patient, they didn't have to wait twenty-four hours to declare him a missing person. It was almost like an amber alert, immediately the police could start looking for Eric.

The search began. Tom, Patti, Grandma, and Grandpa searched high and low in South Beach looking for Eric. They could not find him anywhere. This went long into the night.

When Patti got home, she created a missing person flyer and had five hundred copies printed. She went back down to South Beach, and for four hours, handed out flyers.

She told me she was amazed at the lack of reaction from the people walking by. She was trying to hand out flyers and people reacted as if she was begging for money the way they were ignoring her.

It got later and later and they decided to go home to get a little sleep and resume the search in the morning, knowing that the police were on the case now.

The police also informed Tom and Patti that they would be checking with all the hospitals to see if Eric had been picked up and taken to a hospital.

Not surprisingly, nobody could sleep. They got up early the next day, Sunday, and handed out more flyers in South Beach. Still no information about Eric or any word from the police.

About two o'clock in the afternoon, Patti decided she would call the hospitals herself. She found a hospital where the receptionist said, "Yes, we have an Eric Posey here."

Tom and Patti rushed to the hospital. When they found Eric, he was sleeping and they tried to shake him awake. He was able to open his eyes, but he couldn't talk and was absolutely exhausted.

Apparently somebody had found Eric at 4:00 a.m. Eric thought he was in Chicago. He was clearly confused. The person must have called 911 and the ambulance took him to the hospital.

From 6:00 p.m., when he disappeared, until 4:00 a.m. when he was found, Eric had been wandering the streets of South Beach. TEN HOURS!

Eric could barely walk. His feet were covered with blisters and he was wearing his same old gym shoes that he had forever. He must have walked, and walked, and walked, until he couldn't walk anymore.

The thing about Eric's disability was that if you were just walking, and saw him walking, you wouldn't think twice about him. It was only when you had a conversation with him that you realized something was not quite right. The best I can figure is that while he was walking normally, no one noticed him. It probably wasn't until he started stumbling from exhaustion, or from pain in his feet, that he called attention to himself. Somebody probably went over and started talking to him and discovered that he thought he was in Chicago, realized that he was very confused, and called 911.

When Tom and Patti got to the hospital, Patti said that in the front pocket of his blue jeans, Eric had a heavy, oversized key ring with a single key on it. She had no idea where it came from. It sounded like a restroom key from a gas station. I figured during his ten-hour jaunt, Eric went to a gas station, used the restroom, and just walked away with their giant key chain. Tom and Patti said that the money Eric usually had in his money clip was gone, but there were no receipts in his pocket.

Patti called the Hospice doctor that was on Eric's case and explained what happened. Although he could hardly believe what he was hearing, he said that he would instruct the ER doctors to give Eric a certain amount of liquids and then discharge him back to Tom and Patti.

Tom and Patti showed the hospital doctors and nurses the "Do Not Resuscitate" order and explained to them that Eric was under hospice care.

The hospital personnel were very suspicious of the entire situation and said to Tom, "We're keeping Eric overnight for observation."

Tom said, "I thought the Hospice doctor told you to give him the fluids and release him."

The staff person said, "No, we were told to keep Eric overnight for observation."

Tom called the Hospice doctor again and had him repeat his instructions to release Eric after administering fluids.

Finally, the nurse agreed to release Eric to Tom, but they remained very suspicious.

I was back in Chicago and had no idea any of this was going on. Maggie said they didn't want to tell me until they found Eric so I wouldn't worry. About six o'clock on Sunday evening, when I was on the phone getting the story from Patti and Maggie, their doorbell rang. It was the ambulance bringing Eric back to their house.

When I heard the doorbell in the background I said to Maggie, "He's back!" Of course we can laugh about it now, but I couldn't even imagine what happened in those ten hours of Eric wandering around South Beach, Miami and it will forever remain a mystery.

We joked that Eric finally got his key and went out to the clubs that night in South Beach. We imagined Eric saying, "What part of 'I want to go out to the clubs' don't you people understand?"

Finding the humor helped us cope with the incredible stress we dealt with every day.

Since Tom had to be in Phoenix on Thursday, prior to the South Beach disaster, we booked Eric's ticket to Phoenix so Tom could take Eric out to the Foundation and get him settled. We had a family meeting and agreed to continue with our plan.

Monday, Eric was really feeling the effects of that ten-hour walk around South Beach. He was very, very tired and his feet were still sore and filled with blisters. He tried to stand up a few times, but then realized how badly his feet felt and he would lie back down in bed.

Tuesday was the day that Eric's parents were returning home to Hilton Head. They had already changed their flights two or three times.

Eric slept a lot on Tuesday. He was very tired and as Tom described to me, showed a new level of weakness. Was this just weakness because he had this ten-hour ordeal on South Beach or was this the beginning of the deterioration that the doctors thought was going to start over a month ago? We had no way of knowing. He still had one more day to recover before the trip to Phoenix.

Phoenix

WEDNESDAY, ERIC WAS COMPLETELY EXHAUSTED. They managed to get him up and ready for the flight to Phoenix to begin the rehab program in Arizona. The Hospice nurse came and bathed him. Late that afternoon they got Eric into the car, which was no small feat, and took him to the airport where curb-to-curb wheelchair service was arranged. When Patti requested the wheelchair service, the airline agreed to put Eric in first class so he didn't have to walk very far from the wheelchair to his seat.

On Thursday morning, the 6th, Eric arrived without any problems in Arizona. Luis was there to meet Tom and Eric. They put Eric in the wheelchair, loaded him into the van, and took him back to Luis's house.

Luis and his father headed up to the Five Fingers Foundation and they had several other people living in their home, so Eric had instant housemates. The set-up reminded me of a group home. The residents were all different ages. There was a woman with her kids who were trying to make ends meet and a young man, whom Luis helped and mentored.

Eric had his own bedroom, new furniture, and the ability to make phone calls whenever he wanted. Eric's brother said it was a very warm, welcoming atmosphere and he said Eric seemed comfortable with the situation.

It was so strange for me to be separated from Eric after so many years together and especially after taking care of him during his illness for almost five years. I knew this was our best option for getting Eric the care he needed and at the end of the day, I had to protect Alex and Tommy and I know that if Eric were in his right mind, they would also be his number one priority.

The first few days, Luis and his dad drove Eric around the neighborhood in their van to give him a tour. Eric was weak, but they helped him get around and also set up a chair in the yard for him, while they did yard work. Eric even wanted to participate in board games the group would play in the evenings.

Luis told me that Eric took a liking to the daughter of the woman who lived in the house. The girl had dark hair and was about the same age as our daughter, Alex. He may have confused her with Alex or felt a connection with her because he was thinking of Alex.

I spoke with Eric on the phone each day and he seemed ok. He sounded weak, but was able to converse and told me he was doing fine.

It didn't last. The next few days, Eric lost his appetite and slept a lot.

Luis was going to set up a web cam, so we could see Eric when we spoke with him, which would have been great for Alex and Tommy, but we never got the chance. The first day we were to try it, Eric slept most of the day and we weren't able to talk with him. We agreed we would try the next evening, but around 9:00 a.m. the next day, I got a call from Eric's brother, telling me Eric was not doing well. He was alive, but had been unresponsive to Luis for a few hours.

I called Luis and he repeated what Tom had said. I asked Luis to put the phone next to Eric's ear. I said, "Eric, please open your eyes for Luis. It's me, Wendy. I love you very much and I will be coming there very soon."

When Luis got back on the phone, he said there was no response from Eric. I told Luis I would call him back in thirty minutes. I was going to book an airline ticket to get to Phoenix and I'd call him back in a half hour.

Not ten minutes later the phone rang and it was Tom's wife, Patti. She said, "I'm sorry Wendy. I just hung up with Luis and he said Eric passed away."

I couldn't process the information. Passed away? I knew Eric was sick, but I certainly wasn't ready for that news. *Is anyone ever ready for that news?* My heart was pounding and I felt an echo in my ears. It felt like I was drowning.

I remember calling my brother, Butch, and he seemed to appear at my door instantly. Then other people started to appear at my door and the phone was ringing and all I could think about was, *how was I going to tell Alex and Tommy?*

I had most of the day to sit and take it all in before the kids got home. What made it even more difficult is that I remembered having to tell them about my mom passing away just a few years earlier.

When they came home, I told them I had to talk to them and asked them to sit with me on the couch. I said, "Today is a very sad day. Remember we were going to talk to Daddy last night, but he was sleeping?" They both nodded.

"I got a call from Aunt Patti this morning. She talked to her cousin Luis and he said that Daddy slept the whole night and passed away this morning."

Both kids instantly started sobbing and they buried their little heads in my chest. My heart broke. They certainly were too little to have to go through this.

Through his tears, Tommy asked, "Who am I going to throw the football with now?"

I said, "I know I'm not as good as Daddy at throwing, but I would love to throw the football with you."

They cried for a long time. That night Alex, Tommy and I had a slumber party in my room and we all slept together in my bed. I thought it was important that we were together. I knew we had a busy and emotional week ahead of us.

PART SIX

Saying Goodbye; Gaining
Perspective; Expressing Gratitude

Laughter, the Great Stress Reliever

THE NEXT WEEK WAS FILLED with phone calls and arrangements. We knew we wanted to have a memorial service for Eric. Tom and I visited several area funeral homes and picked one for the service.

I had to finalize some details with the funeral director, so Maureen and I drove over to meet with him. After I parked the van, I glanced in the rearview mirror and saw how ghastly I looked. I hadn't slept very much and looked scary.

I told Maureen that I was going to scare the funeral director with my looks. Then I asked her, "Do I look like a widow?"

What followed was ten minutes of uncontrollable laughter and giggling from the two of us, while we sat in the funeral home parking lot in my van. I'm sure it was all stress related. It reminded me of the Mary Tyler Moore episode when Chuckles The Clown died and Mary couldn't stop her nervous laughing. I told Maureen, "If we go in there laughing hysterically, the guy is going to think we're nuts."

Caring Enough To Send A Card

I WORKED WITH THE KIDS on putting picture boards together of Eric for the memorial service, which was a great celebration of his life. Hundreds of people attended. Many people spoke and shared stories about Eric, including Eric's brother, Tom, and me. I knew I had to speak before anyone else or I'd chicken out. I've included the text of our two speeches in the appendix of this book.

The funeral mass was held at our church. It was sad, wonderful, and comforting, with family and friends surrounding us. The music was incredible.

My friend Art told me that after his dad died, he was very touched by the number of people who sent him sympathy cards and attended his dad's services. From then on, he made it a point to always send cards and attend as many funeral services as he could. This was because of the outpouring of friendship he felt when his dad passed away.

I couldn't agree more. I was so grateful to the people who took the time to send me a card or pay their respects at Eric's services. Alex and Tommy's teachers had their classmates make cards for them. My favorite card was a pretty homemade one, colored in bright crayon, from a little girl in one of my kids' classes who wrote, "I am sorry your Dad pasted away." *Priceless.* I even got a card from Walgreen's pharmacy. *I knew they'd miss us.* One of the cards that fell into the category of "there sure are some nice people in this world" came from a woman in our neighborhood who went to our church. She wrote:

> Dear Wendy,
> Although we have only met one time—when you
> came to see my kitchen based on a neighbor's
> suggestion—I have seen you at church and heard
> about your struggle the past five years. I am so sorry
> to hear about the loss of your husband. Hopefully, you
> will find peace, knowing that he is resting comfortably
> in the arms of his Heavenly Father.

I heard of Eric's death at 9:00 mass, yesterday, and was trying to think of something I could do to ease the pain of being a single parent. I know you enjoy being in the choir, so I would like to offer free babysitting for you to attend practice. I could come or my 15-year-old daughter or 12-year-old son. Please call if this is something you could use.

Sincerely,
Debbie G.

This card touched me so much. The fact that she heard my story and sat in church and thought about how she could help, just blew me away. Her kids now babysit for my children while I go to choir practice. They are great kids. If Alex and Tommy turn out like Debbie's kids, I will be a lucky mom.

I wrote a letter expressing my gratitude to Eric's boss, John, who was so kind in expediting Eric's disability insurance. Here is his response:

April 8, 2008

Dear Wendy,

I received your note the other day and shared it with others here at Management Dynamics who knew Eric. We were all very sad. Thank you for thinking of us and your kind remarks. I also shared your note with my wife last night and it made her cry.

Let me express my sincere condolences for your loss and everything you and your family have been through over the past five years. You are right that none of us knew Eric very long, but I have thought about him from time to time and had hoped his short-term memory loss would return.

I have owned Management Dynamics for eighteen years now. We have always sought to provide the best disability insurance available. While we have only used it twice over that entire time, knowing it provided some relief to you and your children makes me feel it was a very worthy investment.

Sincerely Yours,
John W. Preuninger
President

I remember being so touched when I received this response from John. In life, you cross paths with so many unpleasant people who don't want to be bothered. My whole experience with John made me believe there are still some incredibly nice people in this world.

A Child's Perspective…

RIGHT UP TO THE END, if there was a thunderstorm and the kids were scared, or if they were watching a movie that got a little too scary, they ran right to Eric and sat in his lap for safety. It made me happy that they still thought of Eric as a strong person and their protector. I was glad they weren't 100% aware of his diminished capacity.

The kids seemed to handle the services for Eric well. A month after Eric died, Alex made her first communion. She looked so beautiful in her white dress and she was so excited about her big day.

After the mass, while we were taking pictures, Alex whispered to me, "Mommy, I'm glad Daddy wasn't here for my communion."

When I asked her why, she said, "Because what if he had a seizure right in the middle of it?"

My, oh my, how young minds think! The poor girl had witnessed too much strange behavior from her dad over the course of his illness and felt relieved that he wasn't at her communion.

I told her she was right, it could have happened if he were there. I told her that Daddy was up in heaven with a front row seat watching down as she made her communion, and he was very proud.

A few months after Eric died, I was planting my flowerpots with Tommy's help. I looked over at him and said, "I can't believe that you'll be in first grade next year and you'll be gone all day. I will miss you, but I'm glad that I have Rosie (our dog) to keep me company."

As we filled the pots with dirt, Tommy said very nonchalantly, "Yep, dogs are good. They're good for when your boy goes to first grade; they're good when your husband is dead. Dogs are good."

I looked at Tommy, bit the inside of my cheek so I wouldn't burst out laughing, and nodded in agreement. Out of the mouths of babes. Of course I couldn't wait to call Maggie and tell her this story. Now, every once in a while, one of us will just say out of the blue "Dogs are good."

As far as what effects this ordeal had on our kids, I'm sure we weren't lucky enough to go unscathed. Time will tell. I do think our kids will be more compassionate and understanding toward others for having been on this journey. Whatever issues present themselves, we will deal with them together.

It is too painful to look into the future and think of all the things that Eric won't be around to see - Alex and Tommy going through their school years, college, relationships, weddings and someday starting their own families. He won't be with us in the flesh, but he is, and will always be in our hearts.

Our first Father's Day without Eric. The kids wrote notes to him, tied them to the balloon strings and let the balloons go. It has become a Father's Day tradition.

Family

THE ILLNESS OF A LOVED ONE is very stressful. Through the entire ordeal, I felt like I was in a pressure cooker and sometimes any little thing would set me off. There were family arguments and drama. Everyone had his/her own idea of how things should work or be handled and when people disagreed in the midst of this combustible situation, sparks flew.

At the end of the day, everyone pitched in because that's what families do, and for that I will always be grateful to both sides of my family.

After Eric passed away, I really suffered a huge sense of loss for my mom. I cried for days thinking about her, wishing she were with me. It was as if she just died that day and not three years ago. When I reflected on it, I thought it was weird that my reaction to Eric's death was so monopolized with grief for my mom.

When I shared that with my mother-in-law, she thought it was because I was never fully able to grieve the loss of my mom, since I was in the middle of taking care of Eric. I'm sure that had something to do with it. All I knew was the hole in my heart felt like the Grand Canyon.

On a positive note, this horrible tragedy created a bond between Eric's mom and me that we probably would not have had otherwise. I love and respect her so much and I am blessed to have her in my life and in our kids' lives.

Friends

I AM VERY BLESSED with incredibly great friends. I get a lump in my throat when I think about it. My friends are funny, supportive, and loyal and I know I can count on them, no matter what.

They are great listeners and give good advice. They've been there to share the highlights of my life and they stayed and supported me through the difficult challenges. They have never turned their backs on me or kicked me when I was down. I know I can call them at anytime day or night and they will be there for me. I know it because they've proven it over and over again.

Eric, too, was blessed with great friends. I can't begin to explain the unwavering courage and support these men demonstrated during Eric's illness. They truly cared for Eric, took him out for excursions and most importantly, spent time with him, which was very hard to do because Eric wasn't the same person anymore.

They were such loyal friends and I will always be grateful to these men. I am honored to call them my friends, as well. Our friends have always supported Eric and me and they continue to support me, and the kids, to this day.

Lessons Learned

IN A SITUATION LIKE OURS, hearing those words, "Eric has a mass in his brain," certainly gets your attention. That type of scare is like a slap of reality right across the face. It gives you perspective and teaches you lessons. I have learned so much from this experience. The biggest lesson I learned is that life is too short. It's not worth holding grudges or withholding forgiveness because it hurts you and others. Who knows if you or they will be around tomorrow? I didn't easily come to this conclusion. It was definitely a process.

I also learned not to put things off. Do the things you've always wanted to do because life is unpredictable and you never know what tomorrow will bring. I'm not saying blow your life savings, but appreciate the blessings that are right under your nose.

Take the many opportunities you have now to spend time with your loved ones and do the things you enjoy. I am so glad that I threw Eric a surprise 40th birthday party because who knew four years later, he'd be permanently altered. He was able to enjoy the party and visit with all the people who loved him.

I am grateful I had seven years with Eric to travel and spend quality time together before we had kids. I kept all the birthday cards and Mother's Day cards Eric gave me in the years before he got sick. He wrote so many nice things in them about how much he loved me and how much he appreciated me. It helps me to go back and read those cards now because he was so unaware of his situation when he was sick and he rarely expressed those types of feelings. I am happy I kept them.

I have always taken a lot of pictures and I am thrilled to have so many great photos and videos of Eric. I haven't been able to watch the videos yet, it's just too soon, but I treasure them because the kids will always be able to see their dad and hear his voice, and that is priceless.

We have a dear colleague who was around the same age as Eric when he passed away from cancer. His wife told me that he fought the illness with everything he had, but when he realized that he wasn't going to win the battle, he told her he would have done things a lot differently in his life.

He had been a workaholic and at the end, he told his wife that he would have worked less, gone on more family vacations and spent more time with her and their children.

Haven't you always heard the saying that on their deathbed, nobody ever wished they had spent more time at work? When you're leaving this life, will you be satisfied? Are you living your life now, the way you want to? What will your family and friends remember about you?

I learned how important faith is in my life. My faith pulled me through on the days I didn't think I'd make it. I know God put all the wonderful people in my life when I needed them and I believe he also put the people who disappointed me in my life to teach me and give me perspective.

We sing a song in our choir called "Who Am I." I think it really captures the idea of faith that I am talking about. Here are some of the lyrics:

Who Am I?

Who am I, that the Lord of all the earth would care to know my name, would care to feel my hurt?

Who am I, that the Bright and Morning Star would choose to light the way for my ever wand'ring heart?

I am a flower quickly fading, here today and gone tomorrow; A wave tossed in the ocean, a vapor in the wind. Still, You hear me when I'm calling.

Lord, You catch me when I'm falling. And You've told me who I am: I am Yours.

The Lord caught me when I was falling and helped me get through this difficult ordeal.

I learned that as hard as it is sometimes, you have to ask for help when you need it. People want to help; it's just that they usually don't know what it is they can do.

Finally, I learned that no matter how bad you think you have it, there is ALWAYS someone who has it worse.

Now What?

I MADE IT THROUGH this terrible situation with the help of my family, my awesome friends, my sense of humor and lots of chocolate. Now it's time to figure out, yet again, what our new normal is. I promised Eric that I would raise Alex and Tommy and make him proud, and that is what I intend to do.

The transition to a new life without Eric has been difficult and strange. Things I didn't think would be so hard for me, were. Adjusting to life as a single mom, after being part of a couple for so long, has been difficult. Being the fifth wheel and feeling self-conscious attending events alone weren't things I ever thought about, yet these were the things I found excruciatingly hard in the beginning.

It took me a year to clean out Eric's closet and to delete his cell phone number from my cell's address book. Just recently, I finally took his shampoo out of our shower caddy. And I have to admit, there is still a box of Grape Nuts in our cereal cabinet. What I wouldn't give to sit across from Eric, while he enjoyed a giant bowl of Grape Nuts. I'd sit there until the last slurp! Sometimes the things that annoyed you the most are the things you miss the most.

Recently, our favorite restaurant closed. It was the one that we frequented before we had kids. The diner that we had breakfast in when we decided we were going to adopt our daughter, Alex, closed too. More signs that life changes and time marches on.

At the end of the day, you deal with life's challenges as they come. This terrible thing happened to our family, but I didn't want it to define us. You do the best you can and hope life lays off the curve balls for a while. Until then, I will live life to the fullest, do my best to teach Alex and Tommy to be kind and caring individuals, and try very hard to remember to appreciate the blessings that are right in front of me.

We live next door to a Lutheran church and every few weeks they display a different message on their sign out front. Not long ago, the sign read, "Sorrow looks back, faith looks up." I'm not looking back anymore; from now on, I'm looking up.

APPENDIX

Celebrating Eric

This was my speech at Eric's memorial service:

Celebrating Eric
On Thursday, I told the kids it was a very sad day. Today is also a sad day...
but we've been sad about Eric for five years, so I want this wake service to
serve as a celebration of Eric's life because he was an incredible person – an
incredible son, brother, cousin, an incredible husband, father and friend.

I had the privilege of spending almost 17 years with Eric. I loved so many
things about him:
I loved his deep, booming voice.
I loved his self-deprecating humor.
I loved how smart he was... He knew a lot about a lot of things.
I loved that he sang songs loud and proud, even though he couldn't carry a
tune.

Eric loved life.
He loved to learn.
He loved to read.
He loved to travel.
He loved Hilton Head, South Carolina.
He loved to eat.
He loved telling a story.
He loved the Pittsburgh Steelers and the music of Bruce Springsteen and
Warren Zevon.
He loved golf.
He loved his family and friends and boy, oh boy, did he love his kids.

The day we adopted Alex, we were sitting in the conference room of the
agency signing all the paperwork and Eric was holding Alex on his shoulder.
She was making a cooing noise in his ear and Eric announced to everyone at
the table, "I'll sign anything you put in front of me."

After we adopted Tommy, I remember going home and Eric was sitting in a chair holding Tommy and he said, "I can't believe I'm holding my son."

We both fell in love with those kids instantly.

I've said in the past that everyone has their own idea of what heaven is like. I think it's tailored for every individual person.

For Eric, I think he's up there in heaven, finally, clear minded, with a complete memory and fully aware after so many years of confusion. He'll have 50-yard line seats for every Steelers game and he'll play the gorgeous golf courses of heaven, where every drive is straight and every putt rolls in, and for those of you who have played golf with Eric, you know it will be a new experience for him!

In heaven, Eric is surrounded by loved ones: Aunt Cee, Uncle Jack, Uncle Eric, my mom and dad, our dear friend Judy, and all those who went before him.

Eric is looking down on us, watching Alex and Tommy with great pride and sending all of us, here, the strength we need tonight and in the coming weeks and months to handle whatever challenges are ahead of us.

Times like this reinforce what we all know, but tend to forget in the everyday shuffle of life. At the end of the day, nothing matters more than family and friends you can count on. Eric and I are so blessed to have such great family and friends. Thanks to all of you for all your love and support you've shown us. We are so very grateful.

Before Eric got sick, almost every night before we went to sleep, Eric would say, "Wendy, I love you more than you'll ever know."

Eric, I'm going to raise our kids and make you proud. I miss you so very much and I love you... more than you'll ever know.

My Brother's Keys

TOM TITLED HIS SPEECH, "My Brother's Keys," a reference to Eric constantly searching, in his confusion, for his keys and many other items. When Tom stood up to speak, he was looking all around the podium and the floor of the room for something. I thought maybe he lost his notes and then it dawned on me, he was "searching" just like Eric had for all those years. Here is Tom's speech:

<u>My Brother's Keys</u>
"Have you seen my keys?"

For the past five years, this was the most frequent question my brother asked us. *My* answer was "Eric, *what* keys?".... sometimes just a simple *"No"*... or, most often though, it was, "Eric, you don't *have* any keys"... but over and over, he would ask me, *again and again....*

Now that Eric has passed, I have reflected at length on his recurring question, and I have come to realize that perhaps it wasn't actually a question that he was asking us at all ...perhaps, instead, it was a *suggestion*...

A *suggestion* to:

Have an amazing wife, like Wendy... Someone who is your very best friend, who commits to walk hand in hand down life's twisting trails with you. Who holds you and cares for you... will go through hell and back for you, and with you. Will love you and be faithful to you. Who makes you laugh and sing, and smile, and beam with a pride that only comes from that very special connection. And, who, after giving every ounce of herself to you, even when life is unfair, cruel, at times ugly and uncertain, demurely says that she does it for one simple reason... because if the situation were reversed, she knows, truly, in her heart, that you would have done the exact same for her.

That's key....

Be a father who knows no bounds to the love he feels for his children. Who dreams of having a family of his own and moves mountains to see that dream come true. A father who is a gentle giant, wise and kind, smart, funny and playful and strong, a big ol' teddy bear... worthy of admiration and trust.

Raise Alex to be a beautiful young girl, intelligent and poised, and caring and fun, with lots of friends and lots of playmates. Raise Tommy to be a handsome young lad, who loves sports and Spiderman, and who is very good at Wii, and baseball and basketball, and who, like his father, can name every team, and who is the leader of every team he plays on.

Be a father who goes trick or treating, fills the neighbor's backyard pool, cooks all that great food on the grill, attends both Princess plays and Poopie Parties alike, and puts up the Christmas Tree. And pet Rosie, and love your children more importantly than anything in your life...

That's key....

Be a Son whose parents love and cherish, and feel **deserved** pride in. Be your Dad's joy, a friend and confidant, son, golf buddy and pal. Be the son, and man, your mom always saw you to be. In the early years, the cutest button of a boy, all blond hair and buzz cut, and the most kissable cheeks ever.

Moving from river-town to river-town, Morgantown, Nitro, Wellsburg, Madison, Lafayette, Pittsburgh... being your brother's best friend, playing in the same proverbial foxhole, although you're the one who came out scarred... never complaining, trying new things, always the "Guinner"... Later, grow to be a strong student and lean athlete, star of your teams, walk off game-winning homers in the bottom of the seventh, and a stand out on the wrestling squad... leading Mt.

Lebo on the gridiron... fulfilling a vicarious dream of your mother's by studying a semester abroad in Aix en Provence...mastering French... biking the hills and valleys...drinking the wine...living the life.... returning to Dickinson, to your white hat status and your captaincy of the football team, and earning your degree in International Business Studies. Testing New York, and returning to your roots in Pittsburgh. And every Sunday, **EVERY SINGLE SUNDAY**...calling home.....

That's key....

Have family that you really can't wait to see, and so enjoy being with. Family that lifts you up (*"all my Grandchildren are the Greatest!"*) and keeps you humble...(*"Junior, get the bags!"*)...from Twin Lakes to Dearborn Heights, Mackinaw Island to Harbor Springs (*"Grandfather dropped the beans!"*), Chicago to Des Moines, Lake Tahoe to Jackson Hole to Hilton Head and all the turnpike miles and miles in between (*"anybody up for a game of alphabet?"*), you are such an important part of who, and what, we are as a family. Your boisterous embellishments, your non-stop skewering of mostly me, but definitely Doober... and with plenty of animated shots thrown in of Bob (Edi Ameen) and Dane droppin' trou, Hedley, Uncle Ralph (*"Jiminy Crickets, I said coming about!"*) and Johnny G., Uncle Jack, Brian, Butch and Jack Splat and our entire cast of wonderful characters. Sparing, for the most part, Kathleen, Mary and Barbara, but simply because you knew better than to make too much fun of your big "sisters" ...you were always smart enough to know that... Yet you rarely missed an occasion to be there, to participate, to support and love, and to make it all so much more fun than it probably had the right to be.

Yipes, Stripes!...That's key....

Have Great Friends. Friends like D.R. and Schmude, Teammates first...a Quarterback, Receiver and Center... three guys connected by all touching the ball on a successful play and ended up being lifelong friends. Scattered by geography, but almost like brothers...real guy's guys, guys from the "Burgh," guys that other guys want to hang with.

_248   Wendy L. Posey

Truly *amazing* friends. Have friends that you enjoy sharing real time with…white hats and beer pong, going to the Bulls games, hitting the links, hitting the pubs, parlor games, picnics and barbeques, White Elephants at New Year's Eve parties, golf junkets to Hilton Head, renovations, and yes, dare I say it, even *softball!* Friends like Rick and Don and Tish, Tommy and Judy and Chris Carson, Julie, Maureen, Rob Riechle, Ann, Regina and Katina, and who can even imagine a friend like Luis Diaz, affectionately known as Quique, and his father, Arturo, my wife, Patti's cousin and uncle in Phoenix, who knew Eric only at the very end, but to whom, our family, will always be forever grateful.

And Patti, who gave so much strength and love, ideas and laughs to all, in a time when they were most needed.

Friends that when you are not quite **WHAT** you were, or **WANT** to be, are there **WITH** you, **FOR** you, and enjoying you still. Friends whose backs, you *never* see.

That's key….

Be a Boss and a Leader and a Colleague who sets an example of integrity, honesty, loyalty and commitment. Working toward accomplishment, seeing the jobs through, making sure the ships sail **WHERE** they are meant to sail, holding the cargo they are meant to **HOLD**, and arriving there on time, just as they were meant **TO BE**, and all the while mentoring and motivating, contributing and caring, achieving and, in the end, foregoing your own personal gains and promotion to put your wife, children, family and friends first.

That's key….

You all likely know I'm a pretty classic urban, metrosexual…but I do love me some country songs…I'll spare you the melody, as I was always the "silent singer" in the group…but the lyrics of a recent one go a little like this:

You find out who your friends are
Somebody's gonna drop everything
Run on out to their car
Hit the gas
Get there fast
Never sayin', "What's in it for me?"
Or it's way too far
They just show on up
With their big ol' hearts
You find out who your friends are...

Eric, I know you are here with us, looking down from that better place, and I know, **you know**, that for the past five years, you have *truly* found out who your friends are... if any doubts, all you have to do is take a good, long look around this room, and around this land...

So, little brother, go rest high on that mountain. Be forever Calm, Cool and *Caliscious*.

I don't portend to know why you were taken so soon, or so young. Sometimes life seems simply not fair. But do know that **WE** will always remember **YOU**, and so **YOU** will always live *within* **US**...

And yes...Eric... we *have* seen your keys...

TŌMEX
PUBLISHING

Quick Order Form

Fax orders:
847-358-6242. Send this form.

Telephone orders:
Call 847-989-0750.
Have your credit card ready.

Email orders:
www.tomexpublishing.com

Postal Orders:
Tomex Publishing,
PO Box 1116,
Palatine, IL 60078, USA.
Telephone: 847-989-0750.

Yes, I would like to order
"If You Do Nothing, You'll Die"
One Wife's Story of Love, Brain Surgery,
and The Heartbreaking Aftermath

Quantity _____ **@ $25.95 each**
Sales Tax: Please add 10% for products shipped to Illinois addresses.

Shipping by USPS Priority Mail
U.S.: $4.95 per book.

Payment:

_____ Visa _____ MasterCard

Card number :_____

Name on card: _____ Exp. date: _____

Three digit code on Back of Credit Card: _____

Signature: _____

About The Author

Wendy L. Posey worked in the international import/export industry for eleven years before marrying and starting a family. This is Posey's first book, written in real time, during the course of her experience caring for her husband. Wendy Posey lives in a suburb of Chicago with her two children and their dog Rosie, and is working on her next book.